le mot juste for any occasion

"**Homosexuality** is God's way of insuring that the truly gifted aren't burdened with children."

—SAM AUSTIN, COMPOSER AND LYRICIST

"**Style** is being yourself, but on purpose." —QUENTIN CRISP

"**Homophobia** is the irrational fear that three fags will break into your house and redecorate against your will."

—TOM AMMIANO, COMEDIAN

"**Bisexuality** is not so much a cop-out as a fearful compromise."

—JILL JOHNSTON, WRITER

"**Housework** is like bad sex. Every time I do it, I swear I'll never do it again until company comes."

—FROM THE FILM *CAN'T STOP THE MUSIC*

"**Camp** is a lie that tells the truth." —PHILIP CORE, WRITER

"**Gay people** are like blondes: there're fewer of them, but they have more fun."

—RITA MAE BROWN

BRANDON JUDELL (bjudell@aol.com) is a contributing editor to *Detour* magazine and the lead film critic for Critics Inc. on America Online. His articles have appeared in the *Village Voice*, *The Advocate*, *Art & Antiques*, the *Bay Area Reporter*, and the *New York Daily News*. The host of a weekly radio show on WBAI-FM for nine years, the Manhattan-based writer has recently been anthologized in *Long Road to Freedom*, *Best American Erotica 1996*, and *A Member of the Family*.

"THE GAY QUOTE BOOK"

BRANDON JUDELL

A PLUME BOOK

PLUME
Published by the Penguin Group
Penguin Putnam Inc., 375 Hudson Street, New York, New York 10014, U.S.A.
Penguin Books Ltd, 27 Wrights Lane, London W8 5TZ, England
Penguin Books Australia Ltd, Ringwood, Victoria, Australia
Penguin Books Canada Ltd, 10 Alcorn Avenue, Toronto, Ontario, Canada M4V 3B2
Penguin Books (N.Z.) Ltd, 182–190 Wairau Road, Auckland 10, New Zealand

Penguin Books Ltd, Registered Offices:
Harmondsworth, Middlesex, England

Published by Plume, an imprint of Dutton NAL, a member of Penguin Putnam Inc.
Previously published in a Dutton edition.

First Plume Printing, June, 1998
10 9 8 7 6 5 4 3 2 1

℗ REGISTERED TRADEMARK—MARCA REGISTRADA
The Library of Congress has cataloged the Dutton edition as follows:
Judell, Brandon.
The gay quote book / Brandon Judell.
p. cm.
Includes index.
ISBN 0-525-94185-1 (hc.)
ISBN 0-452-27982-8 (pbk.)
1. Gays—Quotations.   2. Lesbians—Quotations.   3. Homosexuality—Quotations, maxims, etc.
4. Quotations, English.   I. Title.
PN6084.G35J83 1997
306.76'6—dc21   96-53421
CIP

Printed in the United States of America
Original hardcover design by Jesse Cohen

To my mother, Gerda, who deserves a quote book of her own.
To my sister, Linda Diana, who conveyed through her smiles.
To Arthur Bell, who carried a big stick yet never spoke softly.

CONTENTS

Contents

Contents

ACKNOWLEDGMENTS

When I first proposed compiling a book of gay quotes in the late seventies, there were no magazines around like *Out* and no folks like Rex Wockner daily disseminating gay and lesbian news selflessly on the Internet. In fact, there was no Internet. As for our Godfather of Wit, Quentin Crisp, he was yet to meander into our lives with his immense panache. Instead, there were *After Dark* and *Blueboy*, the basic *Advocate*, a few local gay rags, plus Ed Sullivan might still have been writing his column back then. Maybe not.

The book that my congenial agent of the time, Pat Loud of the infamous Loud family, unsuccessfully shopped around was a very different work: definitely more historical, less outré, and less inclusive of lesbian wisdom and sallies. The publisher that represented the bastion of gay publishing at the time held on to the proposal for a year, possibly thinking the time wasn't *ripe* for such an enterprise—as did the few other publishers of gay books at the time.

Well, I'm now *overripe*, and the sky is raining down gay and lesbian quotes. Yes, homosexual wit, outrage, and insight have never been so abundant and available for the picking. I hope you enjoy the results of my gleaning.

But before you start feasting, let me thank everyone who helped me get to this point in my life, plus a few scholars, and also those I have to throw in now so they'll help me out in the future: Barbara and Scott Siegel, magnificent agents and friends; Deirdre Mullane, a fine editor; those handful of men I have had enjoyable sex with; those who left too early because they heard God was having a sale on halos (e.g., Nathan Fain, Tolin Greene, Ira Mer, Frank O'Dowd, Vito Russo, Richard Fried, Michael Rock, Doug Foy, Tally Brown, Brandon DeWilde, Lake Watson); plus those friends and relatives who get hernias saying something halfway pithy every few years (The scholars are included here. See if you can dig them out.): Rosa von Praunheim, Gene Stavis, James Saslow, Rhona Saffer, Evelyn Soloway, Luanne Corff, Stephen Soba, Sherry Brooks, Natalie Lessinger, John Augustine, Chris Durang, Gerit Quealy, Lawrence Mass, Carletta Joy Walker, Arnie Kantrowitz, Steve Stewart, Michael Bronski,

Sasha Alyson, Thomas Avena, Neil Miller, Lynn Witt, Sherry Thomas, Quentin Crisp, Danny Mangin, Paula Bernstein, Daniel J. Sullivan, Brenda Bergman, Doris Toumarkine, Annie Sprinkle, Phillip B. Roth, Wayne Metcalf, Ann Haskell, Eric Marcus, Lillian Faderman, Joan Nestle, Patrick Higgins, Leigh W. Rutledge, Juanita Ramos, Jonathan Ned Katz, Dr. Dan William, Larry Kramer, Jeff Weinstein, Rodger McFarlane, David Beckwith, Lawrence Schubert, Juan Morales, Heidi Soloway, Elaine Sruogis, my tattooed and untattooed nephews and nieces, and truthfully hundreds of others I'd remember now if I had typed this out after ingesting my morning coffee—and not before.

Everyone is only ever talking about themselves.
—DANIEL MACIVOR, PLAYWRIGHT

INTRODUCTION:
WHY SHOULD YOU BUY THIS BOOK?

I got around to putting this book together after being deluged by so much boring conversation at parties, on subways, and in bed. It's hard to be the only interesting person around, so I thought, Why not put together a book of quotes that people can use so they can sound fascinating, too? Yes, with these quotes coming out of your lips, your life will soon no doubt be packed full of pseudo–Noel Coward types and fraudulent Fran Lebowitzes.

I have concentrated mainly on bon mots either voiced or written by gays and lesbians, who, everyone knows, are the cleverest people around now that Erma Bombeck has, sadly, died. Usually, when you don't have kids to raise, it's easier to be clever. Unfortunately, with so many homosexuals becoming parents nowadays, quick-wittedness is on its way to becoming a lost art, while exotic diaper fashion statements are on the rise.

Anyway, I won't swear that everyone in this book is a

gay or lesbian. In fact, it's stacked with heterosexuals. Some pro-gay, some anti-gay, and some portraying lesbians and gays in film. And why not? There are a whole bunch of lesbians and gays portraying straights in real life.

So, to reiterate for legal reasons and in pursuit of some sort of truth, a few of these folks are queer, some are friends of queers, two or three hate queers, five swear they've dated k.d. lang, and six are totally impotent. There are also closet cases, straights who will be queer in their next lifetime, and homos and lesbos we just rather wish were straight. As you can imagine, until the IRS adds a few boxes to check labeled lesbian, homosexual, transgenderist, bisexual, and confused, these matters of identity can be a bit problematic.

In the end, if you are straight and you're in here, mazel tov. If you're queer and actually said something bright and I left you out, buy ten copies of this book so there'll be a need for a sequel, and I'll include you next time.

Mom! Dad! Guess Who's Queer

The world changes in direct proportion to the number of people willing to be honest about their lives.

—ARMISTEAD MAUPIN, WRITER

What better cover for someone like me than total indiscretion?

—RUPERT EVERETT, ACTOR, FROM THE FILM *ANOTHER COUNTRY*

I'm an unspeakable of the Oscar Wilde sort.

—E. M. FORSTER, WRITER, *MAURICE*

It wasn't easy telling my parents that I'm gay. I told them at Thanksgiving. I said, "Mom, would you please pass the gravy to a homosexual?" She passed it to my father. A terrible scene followed.

—BOB SMITH, MEMBER OF THE COMEDY GROUP FUNNY GAY MALES

· ·

We must declare ourselves, become known; allow the world to discover this subterranean life of ours which connects kings and farm boys, artists and clerks. Let them see that the important thing is *not* the object of love but the emotion itself.

—GORE VIDAL, WRITER, *THE CITY AND THE PILLAR*

I wanted to be out so I could relax and be me.

—MELISSA ETHERIDGE, MUSICIAN

I'm not willing to be tolerated. That wounds my love of love and liberty.

—JEAN COCTEAU, WRITER AND DIRECTOR

You know what I'm saying? I don't mind—if you're a friend of mine I don't mind you coming out the closet, but ease out that motherfucker, man. Ease. Just tip out the motherfucker. Look before you crash open the door, man. Take your time.

—MARTIN LAWRENCE, COMIC, FROM HIS BOOK *YOU SO CRAZY*

We can't be content with telling the truth—we must tell the whole truth.

—LYTTON STRACHEY, WRITER

The closet is an awful place to die.

—SIGN AT '79 GAY PRIDE MARCH

Silence kills the soul; it diminishes its possibilities to rise and fly and explore. Silence withers what makes you human. The soul shrinks, until it's nothing.

—MARLON RIGGS, FILMMAKER

Dear Mama . . . I have something to tell you that I guess I better not put off any longer . . . you see, I am a homosexual. I have fought it off for months and maybe years, but it just grows truer.

—LAURA Z. HOBSON, WRITER, *CONSENTING ADULT*

The day we stop resisting our instincts, we'll have learned how to live.

—FEDERICO GARCÍA LORCA, POET AND PLAYWRIGHT

If people want to know about my private life, they're going to have to ask me out on a date and buy me a dinner.

—BRYAN BATT, ACTOR

Outing is a nasty word for telling the truth.

—ARMISTEAD MAUPIN, WRITER

You were older than I, and far better informed. I was very young, and innocent. I knew nothing about homosexuality. I didn't even know that such a thing existed—either between men or between women. You should have told me. You should have warned me. You should have told me about yourself, and have warned me that the same sort of thing was likely to happen to myself. It would have saved us a lot of trouble and misunderstanding. But I simply didn't know.

—VITA SACKVILLE-WEST, WRITER AND POET,
FROM A LETTER TO HER GAY HUSBAND, HAROLD NICOLSON

You cannot demand your rights, civil or otherwise, if you are unwilling to say what you are.

—MERLE MILLER, WRITER

Greatness meant strength. Strength meant masculinity. Masculinity meant heterosexuality. Heterosexuality meant facade. Maintain facade for the world to see. Cheat in the dark abyss of the soul.

—ARTHUR BELL, JOURNALIST, FROM HIS BOOK
KINGS DON'T MEAN A THING: THE JOHN KNIGHT MURDER CASE

I'd rather be a fairy
Rather be extraordinary
Since I have the choice
To play a merry role.
I'd rather be a fairy
Than an ogre, mean and scary
I'd rather be a fairy than a troll.

—BILL RUSSSEL, FROM HIS MUSICAL *FOURTUNE*

I watched my friend Melissa [Etheridge] come out, and she became "the lesbian rock star." I never wanted to be "the lesbian actress." I never wanted to be the spokesperson for the gay community. Ever. I did it for my own truth.

—ELLEN DEGENERES, ACTRESS

Youth (Aspects Both Savory and Less So)

No position is impossible when you're young and healthy.

—JOE ORTON, PLAYWRIGHT, *WHAT THE BUTLER SAW*

When you are a kid, you look at life and you do not have the slightest idea what you're looking at.

—JANE WAGNER, WRITER

But that . . . is the one thing none of us can ever be: a grown-up person.

—TRUMAN CAPOTE, WRITER

Your face reveals a down so light
  A breeze might steal it, or a breath.

—MARTIAL, POET

I remember how being young and Black and gay and lonely felt. A lot of it was fine, feeling I had the truth and the light and the key, but a lot of it was purely hell.

—AUDRE LORDE, WRITER

When I was like sixteen, I was a total chick—I had big hair. I was seen as this attractive girl, and I would get all this attention. And then I just cut off all my hair, and I quit playing that game.

—ANI DIFRANCO, MUSICIAN

Meditation is for people with happy childhoods.

—TAYLOR MEAD, POET, *SON OF ANDY WARHOL*

Childhood comes at a time in your life when you are too young to understand what you are going through. And you're too young to understand that you are too young to understand.

—JANE WAGNER, WRITER, *MY LIFE SO FAR*

Child abuse begins with circumcision.

—RILEY @PLANET.EARTH.ORG, POSTED ON THE INTERNET

As a young woman of fifteen in a nearly coastal Texas town, I didn't recognize love. In a town where humidity bred hostility, I memorized hate.

—EMMA PÉREZ, WRITER

Children begin by loving their parents; after a time they judge them; rarely, if ever, do they forgive them.

—OSCAR WILDE, NOVELIST AND PLAYWRIGHT, *A WOMAN OF NO IMPORTANCE*

Green grapes may be touched, but his ripe chastity will be guarded.

—STRATO, POET

Every gay and lesbian person who has been lucky to survive the turmoil of growing up is a survivor. Survivors always have an obligation to those who will face the same challenges.

—BOB PARIS, BODYBUILDER

If boys didn't exist, I should have to invent them.

—CHRISTOPHER ISHERWOOD, WRITER

JEFFREY: Dad! I am not going to have phone sex with you and Mom!
MOM: Oh, don't be such a stick-in-the-mud. This is your mother. I've bathed you. I changed your diapers.

—PAUL RUDNICK, PLAYWRIGHT, *JEFFREY*

Boys' cocks, Diodore,
have three facets,
or so those who know claim.
Leave them alone and they babble,
let them swell and they cry,
but when a hand jerks them,
those dicks talk.

—STRATO, POET

Why should it be a crime to love someone? No one is being forced into anything. I'm talking about consensual sex. At sixteen you are a man and you know what you are doing. I knew what was I was doing at sixteen. I think most people do.

—JIMMY SOMERVILLE, MUSICIAN

Growing up can take a lifetime.

—JANE WAGNER, WRITER

My son came out and all I got was this lousy T-shirt.

—T-SHIRT AT P-FLAG
(PARENTS AND FRIENDS OF LESBIANS AND GAYS) CONVENTION

Just Wait Until Your Father Gets Home!

Just think: your family are the people most likely to give you the flu.

—JANE WAGNER. WRITER

Why didn't children ever see that they could damage their parents as much as parents could damage and harm children?

—LAURA Z. HOBSON, WRITER, *CONSENTING ADULT*

My dad is where it comes from—he has a huge dick. . . . When I was a little kid, it used to scare me: "Whoa, Dad, put that thing away!"

—JEFF STRYKER, PORN STAR

Things that wouldn't bother you normally often bother you just because it's your parents who are doing it. I once saw my parents "doing it." It was on educational television. But that's not my idea of education, do you agree?
—LIDIA, FROM PLAYWRIGHT CHRISTOPHER DURANG'S *TITANIC*

We love, respect, and support our gay, lesbian, and bisexual children. We denounce and will strongly resist any effort to label them as less than the responsible citizens and caring family members we know them to be.
—P-FLAG BOARD OF DIRECTORS

Mothers are more generous-hearted than reviewers.
—MARTIN DUBERMAN, WRITER, *CURES*

Your father don't approve of the way you live, but that don't mean he don't love you. Lord . . . parents love their children. They can't help it. That's what the Lord put us here for—to love our children and make them miserable. . . . That was a joke.
—LARRY DUPLECHAN, WRITER, *CAPTAIN SWING*

It never occurred to me that anyone I knew would want to have kids. Surely this is one of the advantages of being gay—you don't have to go through that angst.

—BRENT LEDGER, JOURNALIST

My mother is an unrepentant old harridan. At her weakest with the chemo, she managed to remind me that if I lost weight, I might still be able to find a husband.

—JEZANNA IN ALISON BECHDEL'S COMIC STRIP *DYKES TO WATCH OUT FOR*

Why two children from the same family turn out to be gay is a mystery to my husband and me. Do we accept our sons as they are? Definitely! It is what they bring forth as human beings that is important.

—RITA LAUZIER, ASSOCIATE PUBLISHER OF *METROLINE*

I always thought that the one way kids had of getting back at their parents was to do this gender business. It was only kids trying to be outrageous.

—LOU REED, MUSICIAN

My grandmother used to say that if you do good, you'll get good; if you do bad, you'll get bad. My grandmother was wrong.

—ARTHUR BELL, JOURNALIST

You'll like him, Mother. He has a certain James Dean je ne sais quoi.

—COLIN FIRTH, ACTOR, FROM THE FILM *APARTMENT ZERO*

All women become like their mothers. That is their tragedy. No man does. That's his.

—OSCAR WILDE, PLAYWRIGHT, *THE IMPORTANCE OF BEING EARNEST*

If I had to do it over again, I'd be choosier about my parents.

—PORTSIX@AOL.COM, POSTED ON THE INTERNET

It is funny the two things most men are proudest of is the thing that any man can do and doing does in the same way, that is being drunk and being the father of their son.

—GERTRUDE STEIN, WRITER

I come from a very critical family. We are not only critical of each other, but we are critical of ourselves and anyone else who happens to be around. You'd think that with all of us pointing out each other's faults all the time, we'd show some improvement.

—JANE WAGNER, WRITER, *MY LIFE SO FAR*

Queer Is as Queer Does

I think gay people are like blondes: there're fewer of them, but they have more fun.

—RITA MAE BROWN, WRITER

We do not even in the least know the final cause of sexuality. The whole subject is in darkness.

—CHARLES DARWIN, SCIENTIST

Homosexuality is assuredly no advantage, but it is nothing to be ashamed of.

—SIGMUND FREUD, PSYCHOANALYST, *LETTER TO AN AMERICAN MOTHER*

Since the most important element of any concept is that its originating question be appropriately framed, any theory demanding an explanation for homosexuality is a problematic one because it maintains our existence as a category of deviance. I mean, no one is running around trying to figure out why some people like sports, for example.

—SARAH SCHULMAN, WRITER, *MY AMERICAN HISTORY*

Every time two homosexuals get together, there's a parade.

—JACKIE MASON, COMIC

I don't molest children and I don't do windows.

—T-SHIRT AT 1987 MARCH ON WASHINGTON FOR GAY AND LESBIAN RIGHTS

Gay men have no automatic lineage. Unlike straight men, who can be initiated into the rituals of manhood by their fathers and brothers, we must create our own models and our own rites of passage. We self-consciously assume the roles of teacher and student, mentor and protégé . . . and in some instances, master and slave.
—JOHN PRESTON, WRITER, *FLESH AND THE WORD 3*

One way or another, the penalty for being born arithmetically exceptional is that the developing gay man is forced to tap exceptional strengths and creativity to cope with his status and the shame the larger society insists that he feels.
—STANLEY SIEGEL, PSYCHOTHERAPIST, AND ED LOWE, JR., JOURNALIST

A homosexual is a female soul in a male body.
—MAE WEST, ACTRESS

There's no gay way to brush your teeth, wash your clothes, or drive a car.
—JUDY RICHARD, MARKETING AND PUBLIC RELATIONS DIRECTOR
AT SAN JOSE STATE UNIVERSITY

Many people cling to the idea that homosexuality is a choice, because otherwise the Bible would seem illogical. Why would God decree as immoral something that was out of one's control? One couldn't imagine a biblical passage suggesting people are immoral because they are tall or blond or brown-skinned.
—ROBERT L. STEINBECK, WRITER, IN THE *MIAMI HERALD*

Homosexuality is not a four-letter word.
—SIGN AT 1970 GAY PRIDE MARCH

Gay men are accused of a lot of failings in our culture, but the inability to talk about sex is never one of them.
—MICHAEL BRONSKI, GAY ACTIVIST AND WRITER

The "love that dare not speak its name" in this century is such a great affection of an elder for a younger man as there was between David and Jonathan, such as Plato made the very basis of his philosophy, and such as you find in the sonnets of Michelangelo and Shakespeare. It is that deep, spiritual affection that is pure as it is perfect.

—OSCAR WILDE, PLAYWRIGHT, SPEECH DURING HIS TRIAL

To be honest, gay persons are not just plain folk; we are quite extraordinary. . . . We are not—heaven forbid— "the same as" heterosexuals, but are uniquely different with our own positive and lasting contributions to humanity. Some of us are pederasts. Some of us are sado-masochists. Some of us are hustlers. Some of us are frenzied fairies in drag. In other words: we have amongst our ranks—in our culture—a wealth and variety of collectively liberating experience undreamt of by merely mortal heterosexuals. We are Hamlet and his father in heaven and hell, while they are Horatio with his plodding common sense.

—RICTOR NORTON, WRITER

I claim emphatically that the true invert is born and not made.

—RADCLYFFE HALL, WRITER

When I say my brother and his wife are heterosexual, that doesn't mean I'm talking about their sex lives. Likewise, when we say someone is gay, we're talking about *sexual orientation*, not their sexual activity. It's not our fault that *every time* someone says "gay," people think "sex." That's *their* twisted problem.

—VITO RUSSO, FILM HISTORIAN AND GAY ACTIVIST,
LETTER IN THE *VILLAGE VOICE*

Our sexual fantasies are what differentiate us from the heterosexual world.

—DAVID LAURENTS, WRITER, *DRUMMER*

There are no known cures for homosexuality. Faggots have survived Christianity, psychiatry, social ostracism, jail, earth, air, wind and fire, as well as the pink triangle and concentration camps. Nothing can reckon with you if you can reckon with yourself.

—JIM EVERHARD, WRITER, *CURING HOMOSEXUALITY*

The homosexual and the heterosexual are now no longer distinct biological categories; all people are basically bisexual.

—MYRIAM EVERARD, PSYCHOLOGIST/HISTORIAN

Believe it or not, there was a time in my life when I didn't go around announcing I was a faggot.

—MART CROWLEY, PLAYWRIGHT, *THE BOYS IN THE BAND*

You understand that in homosexuality, just as in heterosexuality, there are all shades and degrees, from radiant health to sullen sickness, from simple expansiveness to all the refinements of vice.

—ANDRÉ GIDE, WRITER, *CORYDON*

A History Lesson

What's the difference between the fifties and the nineties? In the nineties, a man walks into a drugstore and states loudly, "I'd like some condoms," then whispers, "and some cigarettes."

—ANONYMOUS, WORLDWIDE WEB

Pumping iron came in when love beads went out, and if Oscar Wilde were alive today, he'd be on a liquid protein diet.

—ARTHUR BELL, JOURNALIST, *KINGS DON'T MEAN A THING: THE JOHN KNIGHT MURDER CASE*

In the fifties, you had to be a Jew to get a girl. In the sixties, you had to be a black to get a girl. In the seventies, you had to be a girl to get a girl.

—MORT SAHL, COMIC

I wonder if Socrates and Plato took a house on Crete during the summer.
—WOODY ALLEN, DIRECTOR, FROM THE FILM *LOVE AND DEATH*

Our ancestors. Our belonging. The future is foretold from the past and the future is only possible because of the past. Without past and future, the present is partial. All time is eternally present and so all time is ours. There is no sense in forgetting and every sense in dreaming. Thus the present is made rich. Thus the present is made whole.

—JEANETTE WINTERSON, WRITER, *THE PASSION*

Those of us born after World War II all too easily think of the prewar years as the dark ages. How awful it must have been to be gay then!
—JACK HART, ANTHOLOGIST, *MY FIRST TIME*

If I believe in anything, rather than God, it's that I am part of something that goes back to *Antigone* and that whatever speaks the truth of our hearts can only make us stronger. We must be the last generation to live in silence.
—PAUL MONETTE, WRITER AND POET, "THE POLITICS OF SILENCE"

In the age of Calvin Klein's steaming hunks, it must be hard for those under forty to realize that there was ever a time when a man was nothing but a suit of clothes—a shirt and tie, shined leather shoes, and a gray, felt hat.

—GORE VIDAL, WRITER

The clergy is no better equipped now to understand the origins of sexuality than it was a century ago to comprehend the origins of life or four centuries ago to fathom the nature of the solar system.

—DEAN HAMER, PH.D., NATIONAL CANCER INSTITUTE, AND PETER COPELAND, JOURNALIST, *THE SCIENCE OF DESIRE*

Human beings are too important to be treated as mere symptoms of the past.

—LYTTON STRACHEY, WRITER, *EMINENT VICTORIANS*

If you go into the Vatican museum, there are thousands of statues of adolescent and prepubescent boys. They've been a major erotic, aesthetic, classic subject for thousands of years. All of a sudden the culture has said that you're not supposed to feel tender toward youthful bodies.

—ALLEN GINSBERG, POET

America the Pretty

I don't mind playing offensive stereotypes, but I *won't* play American.

—SCOTT THOMPSON, ACTOR

Few contemporary cultures are as hostile to homosexuality as America's is.

—MYRON BRENTON, WRITER, *THE AMERICAN MALE*

There oughtn't to be discrimination. Everything ought to be based on potential. Everyone should be treated alike, whether they're black or brown or disabled or homosexual. . . . You watch some of these programs [about gays]. You read some of the material. And you say, "Well, they don't have a choice. Something else happens. Somewhere in the genes, or whatever." I don't know whether it's involuntary or choice. But either way, they have, obviously, civil rights. No discrimination. This is America.

—FORMER SENATE MAJORITY LEADER ROBERT DOLE, WHEN QUESTIONED ON GAY RIGHTS BY THE *NEW YORK TIMES*

....

The more americanized I became, the more inadequate and inferior I felt as a Puerto Rican. My line of thinking was: who wants to be something everyone despises?
—JUANITA RAMOS, WRITER AND ASSISTANT PROFESSOR OF SOCIOLOGY, WOMEN'S STUDIES, AND LATIN AMERICAN STUDIES, "BAYAMÓN, BROOKLYN Y YO"

There are those who love regretting,
There are those who like extremes,
There are those who thrive on chaos
And despair.
There are those who keep forgetting
How the country's built on dreams.
—STEPHEN SONDHEIM, COMPOSER, *ASSASSINS*

There are in the military gay and lesbian and bisexual people of African-American descent already. We have come over a path that with tears has been watered.
—ELIAS FARAJAJE-JONES, REPRESENTATIVE OF THE D.C. COALITION OF BLACK GAY MEN

I had no idea so many people in the United States and Canada were tying each other up.

—ANN LANDERS, COLUMNIST

A small egg pops out of oliver north's ass and breaks in two on the floor. A tiny american flag tumbles out of the egg waving mechanically. The crowd breaks into wild applause as whitney houston steps forward to lead a rousing rendition of the star spangled banner. I wake up. I am in a fever so delirious I am in a patriotic panic. Where, where the fuck at five in the morning could I run and buy a big american flag?

—DAVID WOJNAROWICZ, ARTIST AND WRITER, "SPIRAL"

For us in the American culture, the body and mind have been split. There's something about going through AIDS that makes us understand that the body and mind are connected. I expect dance to be the place where we see this connection exposed first.

—STEPHEN GRECO, WRITER AND EDITOR

[Gay people] pick up on things faster than straight mainstream America does. . . . I think gay kids borrow from homeboys and trendies borrow from gay people.

—FRANK DECARO, JOURNALIST

Ask ten different researchers how many gay/lesbian and bisexual Americans there are and you'll get twelve different opinions. Are we truly one in ten, or are we one in one hundred? The simple fact is that no one knows, and we're not likely to find out anytime soon.

—TONY INCALCATERA, VICE PRESIDENT,
ASSOCIATE RESEARCH DIRECTOR, J. WALTER THOMPSON

Election Day Blues

Miss Manners has come to believe that the basic political division in the society is not between liberals and conservatives but between those who believe that they should have a say in the love lives of strangers and those who do not.

—JUDITH MARTIN (MISS MANNERS), COLUMNIST

Queers of today are the yapping pug at the feet of society barking for attention, but getting kicked to the side and it won't change until we become pit bulls and maul the people who walk above us.

—SJORDAL@ZEUS.TOWSON.EDU, POSTED ON THE INTERNET

I'm watching Hawaii politics rights now, and let me tell ya, if it gets to the point where they legalize gay marriage, I'll be the first in line. I'm totally going to do it. I don't see any reason why not.

—MELISSA ETHERIDGE, MUSICIAN

I don't think homosexuality is normal behavior, and I oppose the codification of gay rights. . . . Actually, I wish the whole issue could be toned down. I wish it could go away, but, of course, I know it can't.

—GEORGE BUSH, FORMER PRESIDENT

People are still asking us what do we lesbians have to do with human rights. We are still explaining that life, justice, memory and resistance are *our* words as much as anyone else's. And that every fight against violence and death is our fight too.

—ALEJANDRA SARDA, SPOKESPERSON FOR
ARGENTINA'S LESBIANAS À LA VISTA

Eradicate the homosexual and fascism will disappear.
—MAXIM GORKY, WRITER, FROM A 1934 *PRAVDA* ARTICLE

Being lesbian or gay today is by definition political.
—MARK BLASIUS, ASSOCIATE PROFESSOR OF POLITICAL SCIENCE, *GAY AND
LESBIAN POLITICS: SEXUALITY AND THE EMERGENCE OF A NEW ETHIC*

We must remember, as queers, that we are the only minority oppressed by law; the sex we have is illegal in half the U.S.
—DAVID LAURENTS, EDITOR AND WRITER,
FROM *DRUMMER* ARTICLE "A PORNOGRAPHIC LEGACY"

What Are Friends For?

SIMPLE INJECTION WILL LET GAY MEN TURN STRAIGHT.
DOCTORS REPORT

—*NATIONAL ENQUIRER* HEADLINE

I know that I speak for the decent and normal citizens of this country when I say to those of you of the leftist, militant, homosexual crowd, take it somewhere else. Get out of the schools. Get out of the churches. Take your dead sickly behavior and keep it to yourselves. Keep your hands to yourselves, keep your tongues to yourselves.

—RUSH LIMBAUGH, TV COMMENTATOR

The anus is an exit, not an entrance.

—MORTON DOWNEY, JR., FORMER TV HOST

....

Since [homosexuals'] equipment is a bit limited, they need a lot more sexual imagination in sex than the average heterosexual couple. The usual homosexual experience is mutual masturbation. It is fast, easy, and requires a minimum amount of equipment. . . . Three to five minutes should be enough for the entire operation.

—DAVID REUBEN, PSYCHOANALYST,
EVERYTHING YOU ALWAYS WANTED TO KNOW ABOUT SEX, 1969

For more than two decades, we have engaged in dangerous denial of the Christian Right's potential by dismissing it as too extreme.

—URVASHI VAID, GAY ACTIVIST

Homosexuals are the festering finger endangering the body and we chop them off.

—ANIAS CHIGWEDERE, MEMBER OF ZIMBABWE PARLIAMENT

'Tis the season when self-proclaimed Christian leaders spread ho-ho-homophobia with holiday cheer.

—WAYNE HOFFMAN, JOURNALIST, *METROLINE*

Poison kills the body, but moral poison kills the soul.
—JAMES DOUGLAS, EDITOR OF THE *SUNDAY EXPRESS,* 1928

They hope to achieve a "shot" of masculinity in the homosexual act. Like the addict, [the homosexual] must have his "fix."
—CHARLES W. SOCARIDES, PSYCHOANALYST, 1960s

Mind you, I don't say every subversive is a homosexual. But a man of low morality is a menace in the government, whatever he is, and they are all tied together.
—NEBRASKA SENATOR KENNETH WHERRY
ON THE COMMUNIST SCARE, 1950s

I've been hit on (by men). And always the same ridiculous line: "Boy, you have nice thighs."
—FORMER CALIFORNIA CONGRESSMAN ROBERT DORNAN

Homosexuality is an abomination. The practices of these people are appalling. . . . Many of the people involved with Adolf Hitler were Satanists; many of them were homosexuals. The two things seem to go together. . . . It is a pathology, it is a sickness.
—PAT ROBERTSON, RELIGIOUS LEADER, QUOTED IN TV COMMERCIAL CREATED BY P-FLAG (PARENTS AND FRIENDS OF LESBIANS AND GAYS)

The Miracle of AIDS Turned Fruits into Vegetables
—BUMPER STICKER SOLD AT THE NATIONAL FEDERATION OF REPUBLICAN WOMEN CONVENTION

Roosevelt—A Chicken in Every Pot; Clinton—A Fag in Every Pup Tent
—ANOTHER BUMPER STICKER SOLD AT THE NATIONAL FEDERATION OF REPUBLICAN WOMEN CONVENTION

Despite gay and lesbian progress in the nineties, we have not seen a decrease in the prevalence or severity of violence against us.
—URVASHI VAID, GAY ACTIVIST, *VIRTUAL EQUALITY*

Sex on the Brain (and Other Anatomical Parts)

Sex happens to be the one subject I can speak about with absolutely no authority whatsoever.
—JUSTIN ROSS, ACTOR, IN THE MOVIE *A CHORUS LINE*

There will be sex after death; we just won't be able to feel it.
—LILY TOMLIN, ACTRESS AND COMIC

Promiscuous homosexuals (outlaws with dual identities—tomorrow they will go to offices and athletic fields, classrooms and construction sites) are the shock troops of the sexual revolution.
—JOHN RECHY, *THE SEXUAL OUTLAW*

Sex was a subject, like geometry, that [he] had once learned and now assumed he'd forgotten.

—PETER CAMERON, WRITER, *THE WEEKEND*, ON A MAN WHO'S RECONSIDERING JOINING LIFE AFTER HIS LOVER DIED FROM AIDS

Sex was always a matter of cultural collision. "Diametrically opposed" was a figure of speech that could elicit a hard on.

—ARTHUR BELL, JOURNALIST, ON A RICH MAN'S ATTRACTION TO HUSTLERS, *KINGS DON'T MEAN A THING: THE JOHN KNIGHT MURDER CASE*

Tonight's top is tomorrow's bottom.

—EDMUND WHITE, WRITER

It is right and good for women to reclaim their bodies, dust off their libidos, and follow their clits into some sexual recreation.

—PAT CALIFIA, SEX-ADVICE COLUMNIST AND WRITER

My joy was unbounded and I cannot imagine it greater, even if love had been added.

—ANDRÉ GIDE, WRITER

Given the usual coldness and fragmentation of community life at present, my hunch is that homosexual promiscuity enriches more lives than it desensitizes.

—PAUL GOODMAN, WRITER

The sex act itself is neither male nor female: it is a human being reaching out for the ultimate in communication with another human being.

—DEL MARTIN AND PHYLLIS LYON, LESBIAN ACTIVISTS, *LESBIAN/WOMAN*

I feel as if I'm nothing but wetness, nothing but the thing between my legs.

—PAT CALIFIA, SEX-ADVICE COLUMNIST AND
WRITER, "THE FINISHING SCHOOL"

Chestnuts roasting on an open fire . . . Jack Frost (that slut!) nipping at your . . . well, you know.

—MARC BERKLEY AND MATTHEW BANK,
PARTY THROWERS AND JOURNALISTS

Pumping iron is like coming, but coming continuously.
—ARNOLD SCHWARZENEGGER, ACTOR,
FROM THE DOCUMENTARY *PUMPING IRON*

My thoughts are confused with death
and it draws so oddly on the sexual
that I am confused
confused to be attracted
by, in effect, my own annihilation.
—THOM GUNN, POET, "IN TIME OF PLAGUE"

Crito, I owe a cock to Asclepius.
Will you repay him?
—SOCRATES, PHILOSOPHER, HIS LAST WORDS

I could not make love to boys without loving them.
—JEAN GENET, WRITER

Lesbians own sex toys, have young lovers, do threesomes with their friends, visit the baths, explore bondage, dress up in frilly fetish underwear and spike heels, buy sexually explicit material, go to movies that have lesbian sex in them, shave each other, use poppers, go to the bar for the specific purpose of getting laid, and buy more Crisco than they need for frying chicken.

—PAT CALIFIA, SEX-ADVICE COLUMNIST AND WRITER

Gossip with its many tongues swears you're not up to
    copulating,
Insists that you are not fucked, what's left for you but
    sucking?

—MARTIAL, POET

He drops his cigarette, forgets to scratch it out,
And heads home to his rented bed
Drunk with other people's sex,
Aware in other rooms and other houses, in the wild,
Of the salty come-togethers of some thousand men.

—DAVID GROFF, POET, "A SCENE OF THE CRIME"

Top and bottom. Many gay men treat these labels like immutable characteristics, as if we are born with a set of keys dangling from one hip or the other.
—JOHN PRESTON, WRITER, *FLESH AND THE WORD 3*

Promiscuity is no longer in. If you're promiscuous, you're out—in a coffin.
—KENNETH ANGER, WRITER AND FILMMAKER

There are only two times in this world when I am happy and selfless and pure. One is when I jack off on paper, and the other is when I empty all the fretfulness of my desire onto a male body.
—TENNESSEE WILLIAMS, PLAYWRIGHT

He is what you desire, if desire must have an object.
—MICHAEL LASSELL, POET, "DESIRE"

Sex was everywhere. The men who handled the vegetables in the outdoor markets, the bus conductors crossing
back and forth over the wide grid of the city, baking
in their seats. The midwesterners, the men from Oregon,
the sailors—so many young men in white hanging around
the corners of the frame. So many arms and legs pending,
only waiting to be engaged.
—MICHAEL GRUMLEY, WRITER, *LIFE DRAWING*

I've had more virgins than you've had crabs.
—RAY SHARKEY, ACTOR, IN THE FILM *SCENES FROM
THE CLASS STRUGGLE IN BEVERLY HILLS*

I'm turned on by people with AIDS far more than HIV
negatives. I'm sure that's politically incorrect, but it frees
my inhibition to know that I don't have to worry about the
possibility of infecting someone else. The sex can be so
much hotter.
—SCOTT O'HARA, FORMER PORN STAR AND WRITER

Even sodomy can be sane and wholesome granted there
is an exchange of genuine feeling.
—D. H. LAWRENCE, WRITER

The next time you see unprotected anal sex in a sex club, remember: Tapping a top on the shoulder and offering him a condom and some lube is a very powerful way to express your affection for a brother.

—MICHAEL CALLEN, MUSICIAN AND AIDS ACTIVIST

You lean that sensational set of buns
  Against the wall . . . why tease
    The stone, which is powerless?

—STRATO, POET

I do not want to see straight people copulating in the park or in public restrooms. And I do not believe that heterosexuals view such acts as theirs by right.

—LARRY KRAMER, SOCIAL COMMENTATOR, ON
THE GAY SEX ACTIVISTS SEX PANIC

Housework is like bad sex. Every time I do it, I swear I'll never do it again until company comes by.

—AN EXTRA IN THE FILM *CAN'T STOP THE MUSIC*

When Life Is a Drag

Drag is dirty work, but someone has to do it!

—CHARLES PIERCE, ACTOR

What a good man she was, and what a kind woman.

—IVAN TURGENEV, WRITER, ON THE DEATH OF GEORGE SAND

I'd like any role that would stretch me, where I was credible. But I'm not about to drag myself up in leather or chiffon.

—ROCK HUDSON, ACTOR

Transsexual dressing is a gay contribution to the realization that we're not a hundred percent masculine or feminine, but a mixture of hormones.

—ALLEN GINSBERG, POET

My tits! Where are my tits?
—REX REED, ACTOR AND CRITIC, IN THE FILM *MYRA BRECKINRIDGE*

Life is a drag, you know—then you become one!
—CHARLES PIERCE, ACTOR

There are easier things in life than being a drag queen. But I ain't got no choice. Try as I may, I just can't walk in flats.
—HARVEY FIERSTEIN, PLAYWRIGHT

I've never understood why people find it so hard to recognize the real person inside of me.
—RUPAUL, SINGER AND ACTOR

Did Mae West invent drag queens, or did drag queens invent Mae West?
—MICHAEL BRONSKI, WRITER

The strange thing about "camp" is that it has become fossilized. The mannerisms have never changed. If I were now to see a woman sitting with her knees clamped together, one hand on her hip and the other lightly touching her back hair, I should think, "Either she scored her last social triumph in 1926 or it is a man in drag."

—QUENTIN CRISP, WRITER

Every man should own one dress—and so should lesbians.

—JANE ADAMS SPAHR, GENDER ACTIVIST

A celebration of life, liberty and the pursuit of big hair.

—TAG LINE FOR *WIGSTOCK THE MOVIE*

There is more to be learned from wearing a dress for a day than there is from wearing a suit for life.

—MARIO MIELI, WRITER, *HOMOSEXUALITY AND LIBERATION*

Drag will become so mainstream that Jay Leno will have a sex-change operation.
—MISS UNDERSTOOD, A DRAG QUEEN PREDICTING THE FUTURE

I always said if I hadn't been a woman I'd have been a drag queen.
—DOLLY PARTON, SINGER AND ACTRESS

Different though the sexes are, they intermix. In every human being a vacillation from one sex to the other takes place, and often it is only the clothes that keep the male or female likeness.
—VIRGINIA WOOLF, WRITER, *ORLANDO*

The world is made by man alone. . . . Do you blame me for wanting to be a man—free to live life as a man in a man-made world? Do you blame me for hating to again resume a woman's clothes and just belong?
—CORA ANDERSON, A.K.A. RALPH KERWINIEO,
A NATIVE AMERICAN WOMAN WHO LIVED AS A MAN (C. 1914)

Those uppity lads in all their lilac drag!
　We'll never get our grip on one of those!
　　They're like blooming fig trees stuck up on a cliff—
　　　food only for vultures and soaring crows.

—STRATO, POET

Camp is a lie that tells the truth.

—PHILIP CORE, WRITER, *CAMP*

Butch, Butcher, and Not So Butch

Honey. I'm more man than you'll ever be and more woman than you'll ever get.

—ANTONIO FARGAS. ACTOR. IN THE FILM *CAR WASH*

There's two things got me puzzled, there's two things I
    don't understand;
That's a mannish-acting woman, and a skipping, twistin'
    woman-acting man.

—BESSIE SMITH, BLUES SINGER

I was real proud that in all those years I never hit another butch woman. See, I loved them too, and I understood their pain and their shame because I was so much like them. I loved the lines etched in their faces and hands and the curves of their work-weary shoulders. Sometimes I looked in the mirror and wondered what I would look like when I was their age. Now I know!

—LESLIE FEINBERG, WRITER AND GENDER ACTIVIST

I . . . raised my right hand and waved the palm-open, finger-wiggling backward wave I'd used from time to time since first seeing Liza Minnelli do it near the end of *Cabaret*. I think it's a smart little gesture.

—LARRY DUPLECHAN, WRITER, *CAPTAIN SWING*

We go back and forth—you're butch, you're femme, you're a gym queen, you're a bulldagger, you're transgressive, you're straight-acting, and on and on and on—and forget that there must be some connection between these interesting details that make us all up.

—SARAH PETTIT, EDITOR, *OUT*

Rough trade—the kind that fought better than truck drivers and swished better than Mae West.
—BRUCE NUGENT, HARLEM RENAISSANCE FIGURE,
DESCRIBING THE TYPICAL SPEAKEASY CLIENTELE

Straight! He's about as straight as the Yellow Brick Road.
—MART CROWLEY, PLAYWRIGHT, *THE BOYS IN THE BAND*

I was the stonest of stone butches and loving every minute of it. My address book was thicker than most people's skins are. I put rows of stars by the best names.
—FRANKIE HUCKLENBROICH, WRITER, *A CRYSTAL DIARY*

Darling, You Look Fabulous!

Style is being yourself, but on purpose.

—QUENTIN CRISP, WRITER

People are starting to ask me about fashion. I love that! Maybe they think the doctor sewed in some fashion sense during my genital-conversion surgery.

—KATE BORNSTEIN, WRITER AND GENDER ACTIVIST

We are so demonstrably in the presence of millions for whom taste is but an obscure, confused, immediate instinct.

—HENRY JAMES, WRITER

Not every gay man you meet will be blessed with good taste and an inherent ability to properly accessorize.

—PHILLIP D. JOHNSON, JOURNALIST

....

Thanks to the silver screen your neurosis has style.
—MART CROWLEY, PLAYWRIGHT, *THE BOYS IN THE BAND*

Remember, my people, there is no shame in being poor . . . only in dressing poorly.
—GEORGE HAMILTON, ACTOR, IN *ZORRO, THE GAY BLADE*

Whatever the public blames you for, cultivate it: it is yourself.
—JEAN COCTEAU, WRITER

Anyone who knows fashion will tell you that the operative word is *accessorize*!
—KATE BORNSTEIN, WRITER AND GENDER ACTIVIST

Beauty Is as Beauty Does

Any man who gets up in the morning and tells the mirror "You're adorable" deserves to come to a bad end.
—CLIVE BARKER, WRITER

You've lost so much weight, your ass looks like Jodie Foster's chin.
—BRONSON PINCHOT, ACTOR, IN THE FILM *IT'S MY PARTY*

If you're gay or lesbian and you're in good physical condition, you're going to enjoy what you're doing ten times more.
—JACK LA LANNE, EXERCISE GURU, ON THE *HOWARD STERN SHOW*

Beautiful men are not like you and me. Their sex isn't hungry, grateful, greedy, or choked with emotion. It expresses emotion. Calmly. Radiantly.

—EDMUND WHITE, WRITER

A very good-looking lad, all right; and that was his ruin. Brought up and disciplined here, he'd probably have become a fabulous actor, but he wasted all his promise and talent in debauchery and is now most likely either dead in a double suicide with some rotten woman or a kept man somewhere.

—NOBUKO ALBERY, WRITER, IN *THE HOUSE OF KANZE*, A SAGA OF THE CREATORS OF NOH THEATER IN FOURTEENTH-CENTURY JAPAN

Two floors above in men's designer sportswear, a Ken doll body-double in a navy blue Paul Smith suit turned to his long-haired friend, a runner-up in the Fabio Look-alike Contest (Brunet Division), and said: "I don't need to work out more, I need cosmetic surgery."

—FRANK DE CARO, JOURNALIST

There were people who were different like me inside. We could all see our reflections in the faces of those who sat in this circle. I looked around. It was hard to say who was a woman, who was a man. Their faces radiated a different kind of beauty than I'd grown up seeing celebrated on television or in magazines. It's a beauty one isn't born with, but must fight to construct at great sacrifice.

—LESLIE FEINBERG, GENDER ACTIVIST AND WRITER

The theory of masochism also sheds light on the pronounced show-business aspect to bodybuilding. . . . The terrible litany of suffering that the bodybuilder inflicts on his body, real enough in its private pain, is always intended for public consummation, whether in the gymnasium with roar and yells, or at contests, sweating and posing with a silent smile.

—MARK SIMPSON, WRITER, *MALE IMPERSONATORS: MEN PERFORMING MASCULINITY*

Orgasms for Sale

The world is full of whores. What it really needs is a good bookkeeper.
—SHELLEY WINTERS, ACTRESS, IN THE FILM OF GENET'S *THE BALCONY*

With the help of a few select publications, anyone can dial a whore.
—ARTHUR BELL, JOURNALIST

Try a boy for a change. You're a rich man. You can afford the luxuries of life.
—JOE ORTON, PLAYWRIGHT, *WHAT THE BUTLER SAW*

Look, mister, someone's made a mistake here. I don't do fags.
—RICHARD GERE, ACTOR, IN THE FILM *AMERICAN GIGOLO*

....

I was kind of a Hershey Bar whore—there wasn't much I wouldn't do for a nickel's worth of chocolate.
—TRUMAN CAPOTE, WRITER, *ANSWERED PRAYERS*

... Believe me, sonny,
That hairy rump won't make you any money.
—CATULLUS, POET

To Hell with the Missionary Position

This morning even my pencil's got your toothmarks.
—MAY SWENSON. WRITER

However gross my desires, I find I shall never satisfy them for the fear of annoying others.
—E. M. FORSTER, WRITER

How to tell a horse from a cowboy: the cowboy is usually the one on top.
—ANONYMOUS

Doesn't that hurt?
—HELEN GURLEY BROWN, *COSMOPOLITAN* EDITOR, ON FISTING

....

I adore strawberries. One feels so wicked eating them out of season.

—MICHAEL GOUGH, ACTOR, IN THE FILM *CARAVAGGIO*

Only people with a profound aversion to bodily fluids could have invented the bidet.

—LISA ALTHER, WRITER, *FIVE MINUTES IN HEAVEN*

Regardless of why, piss has arrived as a visible component of the sexual landscape and is likely to grow in both popularity and acceptance. It's fun, free and safe. So why fight the tide? Jump in. The water's warm.

—DAN GUIDA, PRESIDENT OF WATER BOYS

Sadism, masochism, neuroses, suppressed desires, complexes, all those things which psychoanalysis invents in order to debunk the scruples and ardent aspirations of mankind and their rebirth in secular disguises, are not sufficient to explain them.

—VICTORIA OCAMPO, WRITER

Branding is an extreme practice. It is permanent, risky, difficult to perform well, and hurts like hell.
—NORMAN GREENSTEIN, M.D., COLUMNIST, *DRUMMER*

Oh, God. No man! Please, not my nuts.
—FLEDERMAUS, WRITER AND S&M EXPERT

Everyone who enjoys pornography is a voyeur.
—JOHN PRESTON, WRITER

I Am Lesbian, Hear Me Roar!

There is one woman whom fate has destined for each of us. If we miss her we are saved.

—ANONYMOUS

Let us admit in the privacy of our own society that these things sometimes happen. Sometimes women do like women.

—VIRGINIA WOOLF, WRITER, *A ROOM OF ONE'S OWN*

Women who love women, who choose women to nurture and support and to create a living environment in which to work creatively and independently, are lesbians.

—BLANCHE WIESEN COOK, HISTORIAN

. . . .

They say you've become a lesbian. . . . Is it because you couldn't have children?
—ANTHONY PERKINS, ACTOR, IN THE FILM *TWICE A WOMAN*

I'd've fucked anything, taken anything . . . and I did. I'd take it, suck it, lick it, smoke it, shoot it, drop it, fall in love with it.
—JANIS JOPLIN, MUSICIAN

What a shame that feminine friendship should be unnatural.
—WILLA CATHER, WRITER

There's nothing cozier or safer than a nice little lez-nest.
—TRUMAN CAPOTE, WRITER, *ANSWERED PRAYERS*

We recognized ourselves as exotic sister-outsiders who might gain little from banding together. Perhaps our strength might lay in our fewness, our rarity—on being a black lesbian in the fifties.
—AUDRE LORDE, WRITER, *ZAMI: A NEW SPELLING OF MY NAME*

Yabba Dabba Dykes
—T-SHIRTS FEATURING BETTY RUBBLE AND WILMA FLINTSTONE HUGGING

There is nothing mysterious or magical about lesbian lovemaking. . . . The mystery and the magic come from the person with whom you are making love.
—DEL MARTIN AND PHYLLIS LYON, LESBIAN ACTIVISTS, *LESBIAN/WOMAN*

Lesbians of color should be as visible as possible. We are a part of the movement and are sometimes invisible.
—BANDA GODDARD, MARCHER AT GAY EVENT

The loves of women for each other grow more numerous each day, and I have pondered much why these things were. That so little should be said about them surprises me.
—FRANCES WILLARD, AMERICAN TEMPERANCE LEADER, 1870s

I am not offended in the least to be thought lesbian—it's simply that I am very reticent about my personal life, a little English perhaps.

—DJUNA BARNES, WRITER

Is a lesbian a woman who has sex with other women? . . . Is a lesbian a woman who is committed to another woman? . . . Can a woman be considered a "lesbian" because she wrote passionate, erotic letters to another woman—as Emily Dickinson did to Sue Gilbert, for example—if she would not have used that term to describe herself and it was probably not even in her vocabulary?

—LILLIAN FADERMAN, WRITER, "PREFACE," *CHLOE PLUS OLIVIA*

To play sports with women is to love women, to be passionate about women, to be intimate with women.

—MARIAH BURTON NELSON, PRO BASKETBALL PLAYER

I do not believe anymore in the natural superiority
of the lesbian, the difference between my sisters and me.
Fact is, for all I tell my sisters
I turned out terrific at it myself:
sucking cunt, stroking ego, provoking,
manipulating, comforting, keeping.
Plotting my life around mothering
other women's desperation
the way my sisters
build their lives
around their men.
—DOROTHY ALLISON, WRITER AND POET, "THE WOMEN WHO HATE ME"

Some of the finest women I know, I have kissed. Women
who were lonely, women I didn't know and didn't want to,
but kissed because that was a way to say yes we are still
alive and lovable, though separate.
—JUDY GRAHN, WRITER, "A WOMAN IS TALKING TO DEATH"

So many times we don't know of any other women who feel about women the way we do. Our isolation is compounded by the fact that society, our families and the Church are constantly telling us that women who identify with other women in a sexual or loving manner are either sick, sinners or both.

—JUANITA RAMOS, ASSISTANT PROFESSOR OF SOCIOLOGY,
WOMEN'S STUDIES, AND LATIN AMERICAN STUDIES,
STATE UNIVERSITY OF NEW YORK, BINGHAMTON

How many daughters, mothers, sisters, godmothers, aunts, cousins and best friends have lived and died unknown? Each woman's forced silence was a denial of her existence, as if she never loved another woman, never rejoiced in their union, or cried for her, or waited for her to come home.

—MARIANA ROMO-CARMONA, WRITER

I can think of no better place to have suspense and a real eerie feeling of decadence than a lesbian bar, because lesbians are outlaws, we've always been outlaws and I hope we always stay outlaws, and lesbian bars are our secret hiding places.

—MARY WINGS, WRITER

Get up, unleash your suppleness,
lift off your Chian nightdress
and like a lily leaning into
a spring, bathe in the water.

—SAPPHO, POET

To understand the lesbian as a sexual being, one must understand woman as a sexual being.

—DEL MARTIN AND PHYLLIS LYON, LESBIAN ACTIVISTS, *LESBIAN/WOMAN*

I liked playing a woman who is equal to a man, someone with the same power of seduction, someone who is not vulnerable to being seduced by a man and is therefore totally free.

—JOSIANE BALASKO, DIRECTOR AND ACTRESS

Girls got balls. They're just a little higher up.

—JOAN JETT, MUSICIAN

Things back then were horrible, and I think that because I fought like a man to survive I made it somehow easier for the kids coming out today. I did all their fighting for them. I'm not a rich person. I don't have a lot of money; I don't even have a little money. I would have nothing to leave anybody in this world, but I have that—that I can leave to the kids who are coming out now, who will come out into the future. That I left them a better place to come out into.

—MATTY, IN *BOOTS OF LEATHER, SLIPPERS OF GOLD*

My father, who's supportive, said the most hilarious thing when I told him what I was going to do on the show. He said, "You're not going to go all flamboyant, are ya?" I was like, "Yeah, Dad, I'm going to start wearing leather vests. I'm going to get one of those haircuts that they all have."

—ELLEN DEGENERES, ACTRESS

Spanning the Sexes

Bisexuality is not so much a cop-out as a fearful compromise.

—JILL JOHNSTON, WRITER

I don't think there is such a thing as a precise sexual orientation. I think we're all ambiguous sexually.

—TENNESSEE WILLIAMS, PLAYWRIGHT

My identity as a transsexual lesbian whose female lover is becoming a man is manifest in my fashion statement; both my identity and fashion are based on collage. You know—a little bit from here, a little bit from there? Sort of a cut-and-paste thing.

—KATE BORNSTEIN, WRITER AND GENDER ACTIVIST

I'm probably bi-everything. My whole take on the whole thing is that I like sexuality without prefixes. I think that's really limiting. Do not demand that I fit into your idea.
—MICHAEL STIPE, SINGER, OF R.E.M.

Oh, you mean I'm a homosexual! Of course I am, and heterosexual too, but what's that got to do with my headache?
—EDNA ST. VINCENT MILLAY, POET, HER REPLY TO A PSYCHOANALYST WHO ASKED IF SHE WAS AWARE THAT SHE MIGHT HAVE "AN OCCASIONAL IMPULSE TOWARD A PERSON OF YOUR OWN SEX"

I just don't see why everyone has to be labeled. I just don't think words like homosexual—or gay—do anything for anybody.
—BRUCE NUGENT, WRITER AND HARLEM RENAISSANCE FIGURE

The intuition of those who stand midway between the two sexes is so ruthless, so poignant, so accurate, so deadly as to be in the nature of an added scourge.
—RADCLYFFE HALL, WRITER

I feel like I am so fucking alone in this world right now. I feel like I'm the only vegetarian left, the only vegan in the world left. I feel like all the lesbians are starting to fuck men. All the straight girls want to be lesbians. I'm feeling very alone.

—K. D. LANG, MUSICIAN

I'm a one-woman man, and I've had mine, thank God.
—ALAN BATES, ACTOR, AS THE TITLE CHARACTER IN THE FILM *BUTLEY*

Homosexual, bisexual, heterosexual are twentieth-century terms which, for me, really have very little meaning. I've never, . . . watching life, been able to discern where the barriers were.

—JAMES BALDWIN, WRITER

Following the Straight and Narrow

If you think I'm worried about everyone thinking I'm a fag, you're right.
— JAMES GARNER, ACTOR, IN THE FILM *VICTOR/VICTORIA*

I have been blessed with God's two greatest gifts—to be born English and heterosexual.
— JOHN OSBORNE, PLAYWRIGHT, WHO, AFTER HIS DEATH, WAS DISCOVERED NOT TO HAVE BEEN SO TOTALLY HETEROSEXUAL

What is straight? A line can be straight, or a street, but the human heart, oh, no. It's curved like a road through mountains.
— TENNESSEE WILLIAMS, PLAYWRIGHT, *A STREETCAR NAMED DESIRE*

I don't know how I became heterosexual. I'll try to get over it. I'll see what I can do about it. It's not definite. Just because I have it doesn't mean I'm stuck with it. Gimme a chance.

—JACKIE MASON, COMIC

When the fuck did heterosexuals get the patent on home and love and hearth and family?

—HARVEY FIERSTEIN, PLAYWRIGHT AND ACTOR

I thank Jesus Christ for helping me to like girls.

—TINY TIM, MUSICIAN

In college, I experimented with heterosexuality. I slept with a straight guy. I was really drunk.

—BOB SMITH, COMIC

Most men know where they'd be without their testicles—in the land of hairless chins and falsetto voices. Without these little hormone generators, Rambo would be walking around in high heels and sporting a twenty-four-inch cup.

—KENNETH PURVIS, M.D., PH.D., *THE MALE SEXUAL MACHINE*

I know that sex is just fabulous . . . and heterosexual people have it with the opposite sex; that's sort of my orientation. Others have a different arrangement.

—HELEN GURLEY BROWN, THE ORIGINAL *COSMO* GIRL

Gay truths are different from straight truths. And most of the straight world does not wish to hear gay truths. Because, as all truth should, it often contains hurts enough for everyone.

—LARRY KRAMER, PLAYWRIGHT, *JUST SAY NO*

A straight man, when something bad happens: "Fucking A, man!" A gay man, when something bad happens: "How dreeeeeeadful!" A straight man, when something good happens: "Fucking A, man!" A gay man, when something good happens: "Faaaaabbulous!" A straight man, disgusted: "Fucking A!" A gay man, disgusted: "Puh-leeeze!" A straight man, when his team scores a winning touchdown: "Fucking A!" A gay man, when his team scores a winning touchdown: "Fucking A!"

—MUBARAK DAHIR, COLUMNIST

Between exclusive homosexuality and exclusive heterosexuality, there is every intermediate shading.

—ANDRÉ GIDE, WRITER, *CORYDON*

Men ... are just little boys climbing up on the titty whenever they can.

—DOROTHY ALLISON, WRITER, *BASTARD OUT OF CAROLINA*

I get sick of listening to straight people complain about, "Well, hey, we don't have a heterosexual-pride day. Why do you need a gay-pride day?" I remember when I was a kid I'd always ask my mom: "Why don't we have a Kid's Day? We have a Mother's Day and a Father's Day, but why don't we have a Kid's Day?" My mom would always say, "Every day is Kid's Day." To all those heterosexuals that bitch about gay pride, I say the same thing: "Every day is heterosexual-pride day! Can't you people enjoy your banquet and not piss on those of us enjoying our crumbs over here in the corner?"

—ROB NASH, COMIC

Forget your stereotypes, your fears. Straight people are not what you have been led to believe. They're a wonderfully diverse bunch, though the flamboyant ones hog all the media attention.

—MICHAEL GOFF, FORMER EDITOR-IN-CHIEF OF *OUT*

Men marry because they are tired, women marry because they are curious, and both are disappointed.

—GEORGE SANDERS, ACTOR, IN THE FILM *THE PICTURE OF DORIAN GRAY*

Straight ladies can be very dangerous. They tend to toy with our affections.
—JANE CHAMBERS, PLAYWRIGHT, *LAST SUMMER AT BLUE FISH COVE*

Just try, try, try to open your heart
This world is big enough for some of us
To play a different part
Although they have a tendency to overpopulate
Some of my friends are straight.
—RON ROMANOVSKY, MUSICIAN/LYRICIST

I dated guys. I liked guys. But I knew that I liked girls too. I just didn't know what to do with that. I thought, "If I were a guy I'd go out with her." And then I thought, "Well, I don't want to be a guy, really."
—ELLEN DEGENERES, ACTRESS

The Gender Gap

There is more difference within the sexes than between them.

—IVY COMPTON-BURNETT, WRITER

I know I'm not a man—about that much I'm very clear, and I've come to the conclusion that I'm probably not a woman either, at least not according to a lot of people's rules on this sort of thing. The trouble is, we're living in a world that insists we be one or the other—a world that doesn't bother to tell us exactly what one or the other is.

—KATE BORNSTEIN, GENDER ACTIVIST, *GENDER OUTLAW*

What is sauce for the goose may be sauce for the gander, but is not necessarily sauce for the chicken, the duck, the turkey or the guinea hen.

—ALICE B. TOKLAS, GERTRUDE STEIN'S COMPANION

. . . .

When I see a white, gay man who is a national bank executive and owns a home and cottage, do I see someone from my community, as a Black, femme, lesbian writer, filmmaker and artist? Do I need to? Does he need to see me as someone from his? Does the fact that our daily realities are tremendously different from one another alter our perception when we are confronted with the idea that we, based on who we fuck, are part of the same community?

—ROBERTA MARIE MUNROE, JOURNALIST, TORONTO *XTRA!*

While presently gay men and women share many social problems as well as achievements and joys, their histories have been quite different, and their literature often reflects that difference.

—LILLIAN FADERMAN, WRITER

The women who hate me cut me
as men can't. Men don't count.
I can handle men. Never expected better
of any man anyway.

—DOROTHY ALLISON, WRITER AND POET, "THE WOMEN WHO HATE ME"

L'Amour, L'Amour

The world is rather tiresome, I must say—ladies in love with buggers, buggers in love with womanizers, and the price of coal going up too.
—LYTTON STRACHEY, WRITER, IN A LETTER TO DORA CARRINGTON

[Goddess of love] to you I sacrifice a white goat.
—SAPPHO, POET

Loving you is like living in the war years.
—CHERRIE (LAWRENCE) MORAGA, WRITER

I never wanted to love you
I only wanted to see my face in yours.
—WILLIAM FINN, BROADWAY COMPOSER, *MARCH OF THE FALSETTOS*

....

The next time you feel you have to say "I love you" to someone, say it to yourself—and see if you believe it.
—HARVEY FIERSTEIN, PLAYWRIGHT, *TORCH SONG TRILOGY*

Love is the extra effort that we make in our dealings with those whom we do not like.
—QUENTIN CRISP, WRITER

I'm an Amazon! I can lift up bull elephants above my head. I can slay dragons to win my lady's hand.
—JANE CHAMBERS, PLAYWRIGHT

Entreat me not to leave you or cease following you. Whither thou goest I will go, and whither thou stayest I will stay. Your people will be my people, and your God will be my God. Whither thou diest, I will die, and there will I be buried. May the Lord deal with me severely if I allow anything but death to separate us.
—RUTH TO NAOMI, BOOK OF RUTH

Dear Comrade, you must not forget me, for I shall never you. My love you have in life or death forever.

—WALT WHITMAN, POET

Graveyard love is a love that lasts until both people are dead and buried in the graveyard.

—LISA ALTHER, WRITER

Would it be silly to say I like to think
we're Leonard & Virginia Woolf? Don't worry—
I'll not tell which of us is Virginia.

—WALTA BORAWSKI, POET

Did I survive? I guess I did. But only because I knew I might get home to you.

—LESLIE FEINBERG, WRITER AND GENDER ACTIVIST

How shall I know if my love lose his youth,
  Who never for a day hath left my sight?

—STRATO, POET

Darling, love is more than just sex. I mean, even trolls can have sex. What you need is a boyfriend. Someone to nest with, wake up with, just lie around the beach house with.

—STERLING, IN PAUL RUDNICK'S PLAY *JEFFREY*

If you cannot find it in yourself to love another woman, and that includes physical love, then how can you truly say you care about women's liberation?

—RITA MAE BROWN, WRITER

Love can read the writing on the remotest star.

—OSCAR WILDE, PLAYWRIGHT, IN A LETTER TO LORD ALFRED DOUGLAS

Love has little to do with goodness or propriety, or even sanity, if it comes to that.

—KEVIN BOURKE, WRITER

We did not call it love;
we did not acknowledge its existence;
    it was sacramental and therefore secret.

—HERBERT READ, POET

Love will laugh at Heaven as it laughs at Hell!
—CHARLES BAUDELAIRE, POET

All amours tend to create a dead-end atmosphere.
—COLETTE, WRITER

Oh! I want to put my arms around you. I ache to hold you close. Your ring is a great comfort. I look at it and think she does love me, or I wouldn't be wearing it.
—ELEANOR ROOSEVELT, FORMER FIRST LADY,
IN A LETTER TO LORENA HICKOK

I've been trying today to bring back your face—to remember just how you look. Funny how even the dearest face will fade away in time.
—LORENA "HICK" HICKOK, JOURNALIST,
IN A LETTER TO ELEANOR ROOSEVELT

Resolv'd to sing no songs to-day
but those of manly attachment.
—WALT WHITMAN, POET, *LEAVES OF GRASS*

Love is a babe.

—WILLIAM SHAKESPEARE, PLAYWRIGHT, "SONNET 115"

Loving you has this kind of desperation
to it, like do or die. . . .

—CHERRIE (LAWRENCE) MORAGA, WRITER

Who would I be
If I had not loved you?
How would I know what love is?
God only knows.

—WILLIAM FINN, BROADWAY COMPOSER, *FALSETTOLAND*

Love is love.

—JAMES BALDWIN, WRITER

One and One Makes "Oy Vey!"

My lover asked me if I wanted to have children. I told her I didn't know. but we should keep trying.

—SUZY BERGER. COMIC

Oppression makes curious bedfellows.

—ARTHUR BELL, JOURNALIST

We all have this idealized version of love, but the reality is fighting, passion, bad breath in the morning, and breaking plates.

—BOY GEORGE, MUSICIAN

I crawl into our relationship the way an infant crawls into
an open room
naked and ready to learn.

—GAVIN DILLARD, POET

A house is not a home and sex is not a relationship.
—DENNIS NILSEN, MASS MURDERER

The gay couple became the paradigm for the selfish couple—all dressed up and everywhere to go.
—RICHARD RODRIGUEZ, WRITER

Although [Mamma] may prevent us from becoming man and wife, and I may marry someone else, and marry often, nothing that she can possibly do can alter my eternal devotion to you.
—GWENDOLEN, IN OSCAR WILDE'S *THE IMPORTANCE OF BEING EARNEST*

If I hear one more person say, "Gay men don't have long-term relationships," I think I'll throw up.
—PETR PRONSATI, EDITOR

Do they really think that because we're gay, young, and urban, we don't have the same need for fidelity and intimacy that any other human beings do? When sex is as easy to get as a burger at McDonald's, it ain't too mysterious or marvelous, believe me.
—ANDREW HOLLERAN, WRITER

I desire a person, not a gender.

—MATTHEW EHRLICH, WRITER

Being your slave what should I do but tend,
Upon the hours, and times of your desire?

—WILLIAM SHAKESPEARE, PLAYWRIGHT

Lovers come and lovers go.
Lovers live and die fortissimo.
This is where we take a stand—
Welcome to Falsettoland.

—WILLIAM FINN, BROADWAY COMPOSER, *FALSETTOLAND*

Juventius, my honey, while you played
I stole a little kiss from you. It was
Sweeter than sweet ambrosia.

—CATULLUS, POET

It's not so hard to make him smile
time-consuming perhaps but what else have I to do

—GAVIN DILLARD, POET, *NOTES FROM A MARRIAGE*

Then they lay together, close, hidden and protected by the sound of the rain. The rain came down outside like a blessing, like a wall between them and the world.

—JAMES BALDWIN, WRITER, *ANOTHER COUNTRY*

I thought I was Sir Lancelot and she was my Guinevere. . . . My hand to god I looked at that woman and white picket fences were nailed on my eyes. I looked at her and I wanted to enter a little cottage after a hard day's work at some factory and holler Honey I'm home! I wanted us to buy a poodle and a Volkswagen. I wanted her to start wearing aprons in and high heels out. Diane would cook. I would mow the lawn and dump the trash and change any flat tires on the car. Meanwhile I'd write reams of excellent poetry in the evenings, each word a modest offering to her. I would then preen beneath her fulsome praise. And I'd bury my grateful face between her legs at least nightly. That's how it was going to be for us.

—FRANKIE HUCKLENBROICH, WRITER,
ON WHAT HER DREAM RELATIONSHIP WAS SUPPOSED TO BE LIKE,
"A CRYSTAL DIARY"

Whenever a society wants to demonize a particular group, it prohibits them from marrying.
—CALIFORNIA ASSEMBLYWOMAN SHEILA KUEHL
ON STATE GOVERNMENTS LEGISLATING AGAINST GAY MARRIAGES

Days of Wine and Poses

Cocaine isn't habit-forming. I should know—I've been using it for years.

—TALLULAH BANKHEAD, ACTRESS

Never drank. Never smoked. My only vice is men.
—WILPUTTE ALANSON SHERWOOD, AS QUOTED IN *THE ADVOCATE*,
ON HIS 1,800 SEXUAL EXPERIENCES
(ADMITTED DURING A POLICE INTERROGATION)

I knew I was killing myself. I had no life. I drifted in and out of awareness. The only time I smiled was when I had a straw up my nose or a strip of tin foil in my hand. I bought drugs like I bought designer clothes. It is by God's mercy that I never overdosed.

—BOY GEORGE, MUSICIAN, IN HIS AUTOBIOGRAPHY,
TAKE IT LIKE A MAN

Give me your desiring mouth so I
May savor the honey of the vine,
And bestow upon me when I request wine
The chalice in which your kisses sigh.

—MARTIAL, POET

But you know, years ago everyone drank too much. Now it's drugs. Drinking was much more messy.

—LARRY KRAMER, WRITER, *FAGGOTS*

What a nasty streak you have when you drink. Also when you eat and walk.

—MICHAEL CAINE PLAYING GAY IN NEIL SIMON'S *CALIFORNIA SUITE*

I'm an alcoholic
I'm a drug addict
I'm a homosexual
I'm a genius

—TRUMAN CAPOTE, WRITER

The pleasure of a mouth and hands on a body charged with dope could arguably be worth any pain or complications that are to follow.

—BRUCE BENDERSON, WRITER, *USER*

And You Think You're Depressed!

I'm just a poor soul looking for friendship on this bitch of an earth out in the middle of this bitch of a sea.

—RICHARD, IN PLAYWRIGHT CHRISTOPHER DURANG'S *TITANIC*

You're neither unnatural, nor abominable, nor mad; you're as much a part of what people call nature as anyone else; only you're unexplained as yet—you've not got your niche in creation.

—RADCLYFFE HALL, WRITER, *THE WELL OF LONELINESS*

Find me a boy
With two ocean-blue eyes
And show him no pity.
Take out his eyes,
He never need see
How they eat you alive in this city.

—MARTIN SHERMAN, PLAYWRIGHT, *BENT*

I am suddenly in a frenzy of self-loathing. The mirror does not even reflect a face; it reveals a dilemma. The picture is of an ugly man seeing an ugly man.
—BO HUSTON, WRITER "MEDITATIONS IN ZURICH"

By heterosexuals the life after death is imagined as a world of light, where there is no parting. If there is a heaven for homosexuals, which doesn't seem very likely, it will be poorly lit and full of people they can feel pretty confident they will never have to meet again.
—QUENTIN CRISP, WRITER

The impulse strong enough to make me touch another creature has not yet been born in me.
—T. E. LAWRENCE, BRITISH ADVENTURER, IN A LETTER TO E. M. FORSTER

Please get over the notion that your particular "thing" is something that only the deepest, saddest, the most nobly tortured can know. It ain't. It's just one kind of sex—that's all. And, in my opinion, the universe turns regardless.
—LORRAINE HANSBERRY, PLAYWRIGHT,
THE SIGN IN SIDNEY BRUSTEIN'S WINDOW

There's a hole in the world
Like a great black pit
   and the vermin of the world inhabit it
And its morals aren't worth
   what a pig could spit
And it goes by the name of London.
> —STEPHEN SONDHEIM, COMPOSER, *SWEENEY TODD*

I have secret scars in places you'll never see.
> —WAYNE KOESTENBAUM, WRITER AND POET,
> "HAUNTING TUNE THAT ENDS TOO SOON"

A black woman singing aloud about unhappiness in love with the consciousness that she was outcast because of her race was sure to attract the attention and empathy of gay men.
> —MICHAEL BRONSKI, GAY ACTIVIST AND WRITER, ON WHITE GAY MALES'
> ATTRACTION TO BLACK JAZZ SINGERS, *CULTURE CLASH*

The ashes of too much grief have choked the song of mountains in me.
> —PAUL MONETTE, POET AND WRITER,
> "NEW YEAR'S AT LAWRENCE'S GRAVE"

When in disgrace with Fortune and men's eyes,
I all alone beweep my outcast state,
And trouble deaf heaven with my bootless cries,
And look upon myself and curse my fate.
—WILLIAM SHAKESPEARE, PLAYWRIGHT, "SONNET 29"

What's the use avoiding rats
    and horror, hiding from Cops
        and dentists' drills?
Sombody will invent
    a Buchenwald next door.
—ALLEN GINSBERG, POET, "LAUGHING GAS"

God, Are You Listening?

Homosexuality is God's way of insuring that the truly gifted aren't burdened with children.

—SAM AUSTIN, COMPOSER AND LYRICIST

God . . . we believe; we have told you we believe. . . . We have not denied You, then rise up and defend us. Acknowledge us, oh, God, before the whole world. Give us the right to our existence!

—RADCLYFFE HALL, WRITER, *THE WELL OF LONELINESS*

If America persists in the way it's going, and the Lord doesn't strike us down, He ought to apologize to Sodom and Gomorrah.

—JESSE HELMS, U.S. SENATOR

Those who behave in a homosexual fashion . . . shall not enter the kingdom of God.

—POPE JOHN PAUL II

I asked God to change me so that I would be like other people. However, the harder I prayed the queerer I got. That must have been God's response.

—LEONARD MATLOVICH, GAY ACTIVIST WHO BEGAN THE FIGHT TO OVERTURN U.S. MILITARY POLICY BARRING GAYS AND LESBIANS

I've learned that God doesn't punish people. I've learned that God doesn't dislike homosexuals, like a lot of Christians think. AIDS isn't their fault, just like it isn't my fault. God loves homosexuals as much as He loves everybody else.

—RYAN WHITE, YOUNG AIDS ACTIVIST, MAY 30, 1988

I've never been tempted by God but I like his trappings.

—JEANETTE WINTERSON, WRITER, "THE QUEEN OF SPADES"

Spiritual Leanings

When I tell people [here in France] that one of every three Americans has had a personal conversation with Jesus Christ, they think it's an insane asylum.

—EDMUND WHITE, WRITER

Just think about the things you've seen
The mountains and the oceans
And the prairies in between
Oh, people, can't you see
It's obvious to me
That if there is a god, he's a queen.

—RON ROMANOVSKY, SINGER/SONGWRITER,
"IF THERE IS A GOD (HE'S A QUEEN)"

. . . .

I went to confession. The priest asked me, "What did you and this woman do?" I said, "Well, she sucked my pussy." And the priest said, "Hail Mary!" From then on I became religious.

—JULIA PÉREZ, LESBIAN MOTHER

Moral, like physical, cleanliness is not acquired once and for all; it can only be kept and renewed by a habit of constant watchfulness and discipline.

—VICTORIA OCAMPO, WRITER

Our churches sometimes promote these irrational feelings and behaviors. Like the idea that gay or lesbian people can't take good care of children. Or . . . that gay men will go after any man walking down the street. Well, those are lies.

—FORMER SURGEON GENERAL JOCELYN ELDERS

I never go to confession; God doesn't want us to confess, he wants us to challenge him, but for a while I went into our churches because they were built from the heart. Improbable hearts that I had never understood before. Hearts so full of longing that these old stones still cry out with their ecstasy.
—JEANETTE WINTERSON, WRITER, *THE PASSION*

It is only when she can denounce the idiocy of religious scriptures and legal strictures that bind her and can affirm her Lesbian nature as but a single facet of her whole personality that she can become fully human.
—DEL MARTIN AND PHYLLIS LYON, LESBIAN ACTIVISTS, *LESBIAN/WOMAN*

Give blow jobs instead of sermons. You'd be more honest—and useful.
—FREDERIC GORNY, ACTOR, FROM THE FILM *WILD REEDS*

Religion has sadly become irrelevant, something of a joke, in the lives of many people who reacted against its frequent double-standard moral taboos and insufferably bad theology.
—MALCOLM BOYD, PRIEST, *GAY PRIEST: AN INNER JOURNEY*

The locations, rituals, and myths of Catholicism are fertile ground for the homoerotic imagination: candlelit cloisters, dark wooden booths in which secrets are confessed, stories of self-flagellation and of the "passion" of men being tortured on crosses. And like the armed services, college fraternities, and other sex-segregated institutions, the Catholic priesthood has always been ripe for sexual innuendo. What do all those men *do* together?
—JOHN PRESTON, WRITER, *FLESH AND THE WORD 3*

Demons were simple. They believed in prayer and the potency of holy water. Thus they fled from both. But men—what did men believe?
—CLIVE BARKER, WRITER, *EVERVILLE*

Yes, since endless time the blind and the crippled have been said to possess Buddha's nature in them and to receive His special favor in their lives, for Buddha has chosen them to bear the miseries of the world during their lifetime on this earth.
—NOBUKO ALBERY, WRITER, *THE HOUSE OF KANZE*

That country's been sodomized by religion.
—SAEED JAFFREY, ACTOR, FROM THE FILM *MY BEAUTIFUL LAUNDRETTE*

If there's one thing I hate, it's a pushy priest.
—GEOFFREY LEWIS, ACTOR, FROM THE FILM *LUST IN THE DUST*

Dying to Meet You

Life, like my neck, is too short.

—JANE WAGNER, WRITER, *MY LIFE SO FAR*

We make love and death at the same time. It is literally possible to die of love.

—CAROL MUSKE, POET

I want to expire like an exhaled breath.

—HAROLD BRODKEY, WRITER

I want to commit
suicide but not that
badly.
Most of all I want to fuck
an elusive forest creature.

—TAYLOR MEAD, POET, *ON AMPHETAMINE AND IN EUROPE*

So much memory, so few rememberers.

—EDMUND WHITE, WRITER

I'm a Xerox of my former self.

—DAVID WOJNAROWICZ, WRITER, "SPIRAL"

I am neither impressed, nor frightened of death. . . . The only thing that really saddens me over my demise is that I shall not be there to read the nonsense that will be written about me and my works and my motives. There will be books proving conclusively that I was homosexual and books proving equally conclusively that I was not.

—NOËL COWARD, PLAYWRIGHT, FROM HIS DIARY, MARCH 9, 1955

When your candle burns low, you've got to believe that the last light shows you something besides the progress of darkness.

—TENNESSEE WILLIAMS, PLAYWRIGHT

Sex has gotten a bad name recently, but this book reminds us that sex is something worth dying for.

—EDMUND WHITE, WRITER, IN PREFACE TO
MICHAEL GRUMLEY'S *LIFE DRAWING*

Dead, I'm more alive and dear today to him
from whom death's robbed me, than I was alive.

—MICHELANGELO, ARTIST

Death only uses violence
when there is any kind of resistance,
the rest of the time a slow
weardown will do.

—JUDY GRAHN, POET, "A WOMAN IS TALKING TO DEATH"

They've already got my ovaries, uterus, tubes—if I'm going, I'm going with my hair, guts, breasts, whatever I've got left. I'm going as a person, not as a patient. I'm going wanting to live, not wishing I were dead.

—JANE CHAMBERS, PLAYWRIGHT, *LAST SUMMER AT BLUE FISH COVE*

I long for the mix of the bad old days
The ballgowns and torn-up jeans
And I sing this song
For the souls who've gone
Sweet angels, punks and raging queens.
—BILL RUSSELL, DIRECTOR AND LYRICIST,
"ANGELS, PUNKS AND RAGING QUEENS"

Death is not a friend
But I hope in the end, he
Takes me in his arms and lets me hold
his face
—WILLIAM FINN, BROADWAY COMPOSER, *FALSETTOLAND*

But patience was easy if it was all you had; and it was. He
would wait, and while he waited, name the stars in this
new heaven after the dead, so he would have someone to
confide in as time went by.
—CLIVE BARKER, WRITER AND DIRECTOR, *EVERVILLE*

I have a beautiful address book a friend gave me in 1966. I literally cannot open it again. Ever. It sits on the shelf with over a hundred names crossed out. What is there to say? There are no words. I'll never understand why it happened to us.

—JERRY HERMAN, BROADWAY COMPOSER

Their mind is the mind of death.
They know it, and do not know it,
and they are like me in that
(I know it, and do not know it)
and like the flow of people through this bar.

—THOM GUNN, POET, "IN TIME OF PLAGUE"

There will never be anyone like her in this world or my life [again], and I'll never stop missing her—but of course there is that business of "going on living"—one does it almost unconsciously—something in the cells, I think. Do you think if all the above weren't TRUE, I'd be here? . . . No—I'd be dead, too.

—ELIZABETH BISHOP, POET

Name Dropping

"Do you really know Oscar Wilde?"
"Not personally. but I do know someone who can get you his fax number."
—FROM THE MOVIE *FOUR WEDDINGS AND A FUNERAL*

All those Kennedy men are the same: they're like dogs, they have to pee on every fire hydrant.
—TRUMAN CAPOTE, WRITER, *ANSWERED PRAYERS*

You guys think everybody's gay. You think Tom Cruise is gay. If Tom Cruise was gay, don't you think somebody would have told the tabloids they'd slept with him by now? You think he shoots everyone he sleeps with?
—ROSEANNE, COMEDIAN, AT HER *BITCHFEST* COMEDY SHOW

· ·

Somebody was asking me. Said he thought Richard Nixon was obviously homosexual. I said: "Why do you think that?" He said: "You know, that funny, uncoordinated way he moves." I said: "Yeah, like Nureyev."

—GORE VIDAL, WRITER

I am zonked behind
Marlon Brando who has
a big zonk
   only my friend says
   his zonk is tiny having
   grabbed it
      but that was in cold water

—TAYLOR MEAD, POET AND ACTOR, *ON AMPHETAMINE AND IN EUROPE*

I told Princess Margaret it was too bad she didn't like fags because it meant she would have a very lonely old age. Fags are the only people who are kind to worldly old women.

—TRUMAN CAPOTE, WRITER, *ANSWERED PRAYERS*

Write Any Good Novels Lately?

Writing is one-tenth perspiration and nine-tenths masturbation.
—GARY OLDMAN, AS PLAYWRIGHT JOE ORTON IN THE MOVIE *PRICK UP YOUR EARS*

We do not reflect that it is perhaps as difficult to write a good life as to live one.
—LYTTON STRACHEY, WRITER, IN HIS PREFACE TO *EMINENT VICTORIANS*

And as to experience—well, think how little some good poets have had, or how much some bad ones have.
—ELIZABETH BISHOP, POET

It's rare that we read a book by a handsome man; most writers are so homely that only the best of the lot rate being called "distinguished."
—EDMUND WHITE, WRITER

I often think of a poem as a door that opens into a room where I want to go.

—MINNIE BRUCE PRATT, WRITER,
"ALL THE WOMEN CAUGHT IN FLARING LIGHT"

It's dangerous to be as good a writer as I am.

—HAROLD BRODKEY, WRITER

I raise the question: "Can poetry, mere words joined together, be an effective weapon against AIDS?" I answer yes.

—JOSEPH PAPP, THEATRICAL ENTREPRENEUR

Remarks are not literature.

—GERTRUDE STEIN, WRITER, *THE AUTOBIOGRAPHY OF ALICE B. TOKLAS*

At its worst, gay pornography has all the pitfalls of any genre writing. It is predictable, riddled with tired clichés, written according to lowest-common-denominator formulas. At its best, gay pornography—like gay sexuality in general—subverts the expected and defies common stereotypes.

—JOHN PRESTON, WRITER

One of the strangest things about poets is the way they keep warm by writing to one another all over the world.

—VIRGIL THOMSON, COMPOSER

In literature, homosexuality is always the occasion for detailed grandiloquent justification and scientific reflections, or of obscure unclean explanation mixed up with a sense of guilt, or a weakness which turns out to be bragging. You apologize and then preen yourself upon it.

—VICTORIA OCAMPO, WRITER

Cultivating petunias in a window box with a lover in King of Prussia is not news.

—ARTHUR BELL, *VILLAGE VOICE* COLUMNIST

Unless a writer is extremely old when he dies, in which case he has probably become a neglected institution, his death must always be seen untimely. This is because a real writer is always shifting and changing and searching. The world has many labels for him, of which the most treacherous is the label of Success.
—JAMES BALDWIN, WRITER, *NOBODY KNOWS MY NAME*

Being a poet is one of the unhealthier jobs—no regular hours, so many temptations!
—ELIZABETH BISHOP, POET, IN A LETTER TO ROBERT LOWELL

Only poetry can express the complex depths, the whirlpools of despair, the agony of feeling betrayed, the passion, the nostalgia for youth, the holocaust of dying, the mysterious quality of gay and lesbian love.
—THE RT. REV. PAUL MOORE, JR., BISHOP OF NEW YORK

Pornography is the first place a lot of gay men are exposed to gay sex. It functions as a kind of cookbook for sexual technique and allows us to build a catalog of images of how it can be when males touch each other.
—FRANK BROWNING, AUTHOR, *THE CULTURE OF DESIRE*

I came to believe that a general offensive was about to be made against modern art, an offensive based on the theory that all modern writers, painters, and musicians were homosexuals.

—MALCOLM COWLEY, CRITIC AND POET, ON RECALLING THE HOMOPHOBIC
HATE MAIL HE RECEIVED WHILE EDITING A MAGAZINE, *BROOM*, IN 1920

I want to be a witness to my own time because I've had a sneaking suspicion lately that I'm gonna live a lot longer than most of the people I meet. If I'm gonna be the only one still around to say what happened, I'd better pay close attention now.

—SARAH SCHULMAN, WRITER, *RAT BOHEMIA*

How Highbrow Can You Get!!!

Not too much culture. please. I'm on my holiday.
—GEORGE DE LA PENA. ACTOR. FROM THE FILM *NIJINSKY*

Culture is not on the agenda tonight.
—ARTHUR BELL, JOURNALIST

If you remove all the homosexuals and homosexual influence from what is generally regarded as American culture, you are pretty much left with *Let's Make a Deal*.
—FRAN LEBOWITZ, WRITER

My music transcends sexuality, because I tend to write in a very ambiguous way. It's neither black nor white, male nor female, straight nor gay. Unconditional love knows no boundaries.

—SEAL, MUSICIAN

I see myself as a sexual surrealist. If I have any message in my work, it's explore your own—especially your sexual fantasies—because if you stifle them, you stifle some part of your creativity.

—ARLENE SANDLER, FILMMAKER

A lot of people's lives get in the way of their TV viewing.
—MARK LAMOS, ACTOR, FROM THE FILM *LONGTIME COMPANION*

I think that the purpose of flesh is to disguise physical function, the purpose of art to deconstruct the camouflage, the purpose of sex to slash the canvas.

—MICHAEL LASSELL, POET

I . . . wanted to be an actor because I thought I could meet queers.

—SIR IAN MCKELLEN, ACTOR

Theater today is polite and boring. Compared with what's available everywhere else—movies, television, fiction, nonfiction, rock videos, magazines, street corners, Central Park, even journalism and daily newspapers—theater is terribly polite and boring. No wonder audiences stay away in droves.

—LARRY KRAMER, PLAYWRIGHT, *JUST SAY NO*

Hate the critics? I have nothing but compassion for them. How can I hate the crippled, the mentally deficient, and the dead?

—ALBERT FINNEY, ACTOR, FROM THE FILM *THE DRESSER*

I mourn the loss of individual artists, whose fruits I was just beginning to know. But I'm not worried that all artists are going to die.

—STEPHEN GRECO, WRITER

The music is all. People should die for it. People are dying for everything else, so why not for music? It saves more lives.

—LOU REED, MUSICIAN

Just because we're gay doesn't mean you are going to like our music.

—ANDY BELL, MUSICIAN

My sexuality does not drive me to paint. A lot of other factors do.

—MICHAEL T. SMITH, ARTIST

The Muses have made me happy in my lifetime, and when I die I shall never be forgotten.

—SAPPHO, POET

Get Packing

All roads lead to Sodom.

—EVELYN WAUGH, BRITISH NOVELIST

I came to Europe to get culture. Is this culture I'm getting? Then I might as well go back to Greenwich Village and rot there.

—DJUNA BARNES, AMERICAN EXPATRIATE WRITER,
ON ARRIVING IN HER NEWLY ADOPTED HOME

In France there's not a real gay community. People don't talk to each other; everyone lives in a kind of isolation. You're alone with your AIDS. You talk about it to yourself, that's it.

—EDMUND WHITE, WRITER

. . . .

I was more familiar with Africa than I was with my own body until I was fifteen.
—BERYL REID, ACTRESS, FROM JOE ORTON'S *ENTERTAINING MR. SLOANE*

A weather change; showers—an enlivening spray dispelling Manhattan's heat-wave stench. Not that anything could ever get rid of the jockstrap and Lysol aromas here at my beloved Y.M.C.A.
—TRUMAN CAPOTE, WRITER, *ANSWERED PRAYERS*

The French would eat anything that couldn't outrun them.
—LISA ALTHER, WRITER, *FIVE MINUTES IN HEAVEN*

There are already far too many people in Washington who confuse themselves with the monuments.
—U.S. REPRESENTATIVE GERRY STUDDS

When I was a wee boylicious thing, the bathrooms of Harvard birthed my lust. I have not been able to have horizontal sex since.
—SANDI DUBOWSKI, VIDEO MAKER AND WRITER

I never feel safe anywhere in New York. With anyone. Particularly the rich people. Otherwise you're dead in this town. You have to watch your step at all times.

—KENNETH ANGER, WRITER

Do the British have a special talent for *such* passion?

—PAUL FUSSELL, WRITER, *THE GREAT WAR AND MODERN MEMORY*

For Paris is, according to its legend, the city where everyone loses his head, and his morals, lives through at least one *histoire d'amour*, ceases, quite, to arrive anywhere on time, and thumbs his nose at the Puritans—the city, in brief, where all become drunken on the fine old air of freedom.

—JAMES BALDWIN, WRITER, *NOTES OF A NATIVE SON*

I was in love with Harlem long before I got there.

—LANGSTON HUGHES, POET

There were a lot more than good buys at Kmart. There was the ambiance. High overhead fluorescent lights flooded the pastel pink and green fixtures as we walked across the beige linoleum floor. Convenient parking and pleasant sliding doors gave way to the thrill of knowing that whatever we came to buy would soon be forgotten as we fell under that imperceptible Kmart spell.

—MICHAEL LANE AND JIM CROTTY, TRAVEL WRITERS, *MAD MONKS ON THE ROAD*

If you're one in a million, there are ten of you in New York.

—JULIE@DRYCAS.CLUB.CC.CMU.EDU, POSTED ON THE INTERNET

Everyone in Paris talks about love, but only two hundred people actually do it.

—LISA ALTHER, WRITER, *FIVE MINUTES IN HEAVEN*

Going Hollywood

Is that a tan or Ava Gardner's *Show Boat* makeup?
—BRONSON PINCHOT, ACTOR, IN THE FILM *IT'S MY PARTY*

She loved to smell Hollywood more than any other place we have been.
—LARS EIGHNER, WRITER, ABOUT HIS DOG, IN *TRAVELS WITH LIZABETH*

If you watch carefully you'll see that my best performing comes when I have my clothes off. When I'm dressed I really don't give very good performances. . . . Next time you see a film where I'm naked, watch my face and you'll see what I mean.

—JOE DALLESANDRO, ACTOR

Have you seen *Bar Girls*? Why do they cast heterosexual women in these roles? When two straight women kiss, they always appear to be spitting up each other's mouths. Is it me, or is there a lot of really big hair in this movie? Why? Are there no butches in the lesbian community? Exactly what do two femmes do in bed? Each other's makeup?
—LEA DELARIA, COMIC

You know, man is the only animal clever enough to build the Empire State Building and stupid enough to jump off it.
—ROCK HUDSON, ACTOR, FROM THE FILM *COME SEPTEMBER*

I noticed that men get all the best roles in movies, so I gave myself the role of man.
—JOSIANE BALASKO, ACTRESS AND DIRECTOR, ON THE FILM *FRENCH TWIST*

Like the vast majority of men I've had several homo-sexual experiences and I'm not remotely ashamed of it.
—MARLON BRANDO, ACTOR, *CINE-REVUE*, 1975

Frankly, you're beginning to smell, and that's a handicap for a stud in New York.
—DUSTIN HOFFMAN, ACTOR, FROM THE FILM *MIDNIGHT COWBOY*

I had to crown *Batman Forever* as the gayest straight movie in the history of cinema. . . . I haven't seen this many men wearing blackened cowhide and sporting facial and/or body piercing since the International Mr. Leather Convention was in Chicago.
—RICHARD ROEPER, JOURNALIST

They used to photograph Shirley Temple through gauze. They should photograph me through linoleum.
—TALLULAH BANKHEAD, ACTRESS

If life is a movie, someday you'll look back at this footage and wish you had had a good hairdresser.
—CAROLINE AZAR, ACTRESS, FROM THE FILM *NO SKIN OFF MY ASS*

Would I show my pee-pee? If I had to, I could. If that's the hardest thing I had to do on film, I would be a lucky man. But I wouldn't want to do any gratuitous pee-pee showing.
—KEANU REEVES, ACTOR, ON FULL-FRONTAL NUDITY ON SCREEN

Watch out—he prefers the banana to the fig.
—EXTRA IN *PASOLINI'S ARABIAN NIGHTS*

You are cordially invited to a wedding where everyone wants to kiss the bride . . . except the groom.
—TAG LINE FOR *THE WEDDING BANQUET*

Ted Casablanca is not a fag and I'm the dame to prove it.
—PATTY DUKE, ACTRESS, FROM THE FILM *VALLEY OF THE DOLLS*

Everyone knows about everybody in Hollywood—who sleeps with whom, who does it standing on his head or in the dentist's chair. And some of those guys just don't like fairies.

—ROCK HUDSON, ACTOR

I don't know if you have a boyfriend or girlfriend, but if you have some free time, maybe we can have dinner?
—NICOLAS CAGE, ACTOR, FROM THE FILM *LEAVING LAS VEGAS*

Don't let your mouth get you into something your ass can't handle.
—LEONARDO DICAPRIO, ACTOR, FROM THE FILM *THE BASKETBALL DIARIES*

Holy shit! Your hair has a hard-on.
—BETTE MIDLER, ACTRESS, FROM THE FILM *THE ROSE*

They say the navy makes men. Well, I'm living proof. They made me.
—GEORGE HAMILTON, ACTOR, FROM THE FILM *ZORRO, THE GAY BLADE*

I don't usually go out with boys. But with his looks, sure . . . sure . . .
—PAUL NEWMAN ON JAMES DEAN DURING THEIR
EAST OF EDEN SCREEN TEST WHEN ASKED BY THE DIRECTOR,
"PAUL, DO YOU THINK JIMMY WILL APPEAL TO THE BOBBY-SOXERS?"

I'm a murderer and a stud! I get to do everything.
—ROCK HUDSON, ACTOR, ON THE FILM *PRETTY MAIDS ALL IN A ROW*

Take That, Swine!

Your parents should have thought of the overpopulation problem.

—CHARLES LUDLAM, PLAYWRIGHT, *HOT ICE*

Fuck him. I hope he dies.

—ROCK HUDSON, ACTOR, ONE OF HIS FAVORITE EXPRESSIONS

You made love to pieces of white bread, you stupid man, and not only that, but I made your toast out of it in the morning. HAH! I trust you'll be more careful next time I say something is just marmalade.

—VICTORIA IN PLAYWRIGHT CHRISTOPHER DURANG'S *TITANIC*, EXPLAINING TO HER SEX PARTNER WHAT HE WAS ACTUALLY HAVING SEX WITH THE PREVIOUS NIGHT

If i had a gift to give you it would be the gift of loneliness
—GAVIN DILLARD, POET, "THE GIFT"

You should never cross a Greek. We're fair but we're merciless.
—ERIC ROBERTS, ACTOR, IN THE FILM *IT'S MY PARTY*

Straight boy,
Don't laugh
Don't cry,
Just DIE!!!
—SJORDAL@ZEUS.TOWSON.EDU, POSTED ON THE INTERNET

Swine! How dare you enter my room without knocking? [Lashes whip] Have you forgotten the House of Pain?
—BLUEBEARD, IN CHARLES LUDLAM'S PLAY *BLUEBEARD*

I put on a Billie Holiday record, "Strange Fruit." Yes, I was being vindictive.
—JAMES BALDWIN, WRITER, *TELL ME HOW LONG THE TRAIN'S BEEN GONE*

He has every characteristic of a dog . . . except loyalty.
—BRONSON PINCHOT, ACTOR, FROM THE FILM *IT'S MY PARTY*

He had the sort of face that once seen is never remembered.
—OSCAR WILDE, PLAYWRIGHT

You're a selfish, inconsiderate, self-centered, stereo-typical, aging, immature queen. No wonder you don't have any friends. Yes, all that because you won't bring a goddamn record album over here or let me come over there and get it! Besides, the Maria Callas Lisbon *Traviata* is not just another goddamn record album. Right now, at this particular moment in my not so terrific life, it's probably the most goddamn important thing in the world to me, but I wouldn't expect an insensitive faggot whose idea of a good time is sitting around listening to Angela Lansbury shrieking on about "The Worst Pies in London" like yourself to understand what I'm talking about. I'm not surprised you don't like opera. People like you don't like life.
—MENDY, FROM TERRENCE MCNALLY'S PLAY *THE LISBON TRAVIATA*

You've sentenced me to the racks, the screws, the whips
Reserved by Love for the tormented lover.

—CATULLUS, POET

What do you mean, since when did I become such a
radical fairy! . . . Since I started knowing twits like you,
you twit!

—FOPPY, FROM LARRY KRAMER'S PLAY *JUST SAY NO*

The English country gentleman galloping after a fox—
the unspeakable in full pursuit of the uneatable.

—OSCAR WILDE, PLAYWRIGHT, *A WOMAN OF NO IMPORTANCE*

It's not that I object to your being a bastard. Don't get me
wrong there. It's your being such a stupid bastard that I
object to.

—GORE VIDAL, SCREENWRITER, *THE BEST MAN*

God,
Grant me the serenity to accept things I cannot change,
The courage to change the things I can,
And . . . the wisdom to hide the bodies of those people I
   had to kill.

—ILENA@CONNECTNET.COM, POSTED ON THE INTERNET

Don't fuck with me, fellas! This ain't my first time at the
rodeo.

—FAYE DUNAWAY, ACTRESS, AS JOAN CRAWFORD
IN THE FILM *MOMMIE DEAREST*

Help! I've Fallen and I Can't Get Up

The only thing I regret about my past is the length of it. If I had to live over again, I'd make the same mistakes, only sooner.

—TALLULAH BANKHEAD, ACTRESS

I'm aging as well as a beach party movie.

—HARVEY FIERSTEIN, PLAYWRIGHT, *TORCH SONG TRILOGY*

It is little enough to crow about, just making it to sixty-two. But I think it is better to be alive than dead.

—MARK MERLIS, WRITER, *AMERICAN STUDIES*

If last night you were still a boy,
How can you be a man this morning?

—MARTIAL, POET

Please, please don't talk about old age so much, my dear old friend! You are giving me the creeps.
—ELIZABETH BISHOP, POET, LETTER TO ROBERT LOWELL

There's nothing more inconvenient than an old queen with a head cold.
—ROBERT PRESTON, ACTOR, FROM THE FILM *VICTOR/VICTORIA*

The more hair I lose, the more head I get.
—MARTIN AMIS, WRITER, A SLOGAN ON A T-SHIRT
IN HIS "STRAIGHT FICTION"

Since we're not young, weeks have to do time for years of missing each other.
—ADRIENNE RICH, POET, *TWENTY-ONE LOVE POEMS*

You shall get young as I lick your stomach
—AUDRE LORDE, POET, "MEET"

Nothing is sadder than an old queen.
—FOLKLORE

What [older men] may have lost in terms of firmness of muscle or dewiness of skin they have gained in technique and versatility and sexual worldliness
—DR. CHARLES SILVERSTEIN AND EDMUND WHITE, *THE JOY OF GAY SEX*

In spite of aches & pains, I really don't feel much different than I did at thirty-five and I certainly am a great deal happier, most of the time.... I just won't feel ancient.
—ELIZABETH BISHOP, POET, LETTER TO ROBERT LOWELL

Nicander, ooh, your leg's got hairs!
Watch they don't creep up in your arse.
Because, darling, if they do, you'll soon know
How the lovers flee you, and years go.

—ALKAIOS, POET

That's no love handle, that's a hate handle.
—ALAN ROSENBERG, ACTOR, IN THE FILM *HAPPY BIRTHDAY, GEMINI*

If I Were a Rich Man (and Other Positive Thoughts)

I used to try to make something special out of the day. But I found it was taking up too much of the day.
—JANE WAGNER, WRITER

I do want to get rich but I never want to do what there is to get rich.
—GERTRUDE STEIN, WRITER, *EVERYBODY'S AUTOBIOGRAPHY*

The trouble with being in the rat race is that even if you win, you're still a rat.
—LILY TOMLIN, ACTRESS AND COMIC

It's lavish, but I call it home.
—CLIFTON WEBB, ACTOR, FROM THE FILM *LAURA*

As Pascal says, if you manage to be well-born it saves you thirty years.

—ELIZABETH BISHOP, POET

HAPPY GAYS ARE HERE AGAIN

—GAY BUTTON

Dreams and Nightmares, Nightmares and Dreams

At your age? Dream on, Mary. All the good men are either taken, or they've dated each of your seventeen best friends.

—ERIC ORNER, CARTOONIST,
THE MOSTLY UNFABULOUS SOCIAL LIFE OF ETHAN GREEN

August is not for loving. Neither are dreams.

—MICHAEL LASSELL, POET, "THE IDES OF AUGUST"

I had mine removed surgically under general anesthesia, but to have it bitten off in a Buick—it's a nightmare.

—JOHN LITHGOW, ACTOR, FROM THE FILM
THE WORLD ACCORDING TO GARP

I'm the one the boys all wanted
An A-list party queen
Now a ghost they've all forgotten
The nightmare of their dreams
—JOHN GREYSON AND GLENN SCHELLENBERG, SONGWRITERS,
"JUST LIKE SCHEHERAZADE" FROM THE FILM *ZERO PATIENCE*

My nights are rich with mystery, my dreams breathless
with expectation.
—JANE CHAMBERS, PLAYWRIGHT, *LAST SUMMER AT BLUE FISH COVE*

A Little Self-appraisal

In my case, self-absorption is completely justified.
—CLIFTON WEBB, ACTOR, FROM THE FILM *LAURA*

I shouldn't be so selfish. If I weren't so selfish, I wouldn't need to be so generous at Christmas.
—DORIC WILSON, PLAYWRIGHT, *A PERFECT RELATIONSHIP*

It takes a lot of time to be a genius, you have to sit around so much doing nothing, really doing nothing.
—GERTRUDE STEIN, WRITER, *EVERYBODY'S AUTOBIOGRAPHY*

I'm as pure as driven slush.
—TALLULAH BANKHEAD, ACTRESS

· ·

My taste is impeccable, even when it's bad.
—ALAN BATES, ACTOR, FROM THE FILM *NIJINSKY*

The minute you or anybody else knows what you are you are not it, you are what you or anybody else knows you are and as everything is made up of finding out what you are it is extraordinarily difficult not to know what you are and yet to be that thing.
—GERTRUDE STEIN, WRITER

In Search of Self-esteem

It is better to be hated for what one is than to be loved for what one isn't.

—ANDRÉ GIDE, WRITER

I've never wanted to be a hero, but on the other hand I am not anxious to cultivate cowardice.

—GERTRUDE STEIN, WRITER, *ADELE*

There's nothing I need from anyone except love and respect, and anyone who can't give me those two things has no place in my life.

—HARVEY FIERSTEIN, PLAYWRIGHT, *TORCH SONG TRILOGY*

· ·

I've managed to face the . . . gay world without the benefit of the physical assets its denizens are expected to prize, but I've had my own wonderful time.
—ARNIE KANTROWITZ, SOCIAL COMMENTATOR AND WRITER

Dogs, cats, kids, I had never had anything dependent upon me; it was too time-consuming a chore just changing my own diapers.
—TRUMAN CAPOTE, WRITER

To feel guilt is to feel wrong, inferior, and we try to keep secret our guilts and our inferiorities, whether we have defined them for ourselves, or received them as definitions from the society we inhabit.
—WILLIAM DICKEY, POET

Anyone who can swallow two Snow Balls and a Ding Dong shouldn't have any problem with pride.
—STEVE GUTTENBERG, ACTOR, FROM THE FILM *CAN'T STOP THE MUSIC*

I admire people who self-destruct. . . . They take control. They are refusing to continue with unhappiness, which shows tremendous self-will.

—MORRISEY, MUSICIAN, ON KURT COBAIN'S SUICIDE

Life, as I had come to know it, had made me nervous.

—LOU REED, MUSICIAN

I can't play a loser: I don't look like one.

—ROCK HUDSON, ACTOR

That big, lumpy Rock Hudson.

—JAMES DEAN, ACTOR

Everybody knows if you are too careful you are so occupied in being careful that you are sure to stumble over something.

—GERTRUDE STEIN, WRITER

A fate is not a vice.
—PETER GAY, HISTORIAN, ON MARCEL PROUST'S
DEPICTION OF HOMOSEXUALS

After the gay man has gained strength, independence, confidence, and pride in himself, mainly through his political, emotional, and social alignment with the sometimes combative gay subculture of the larger community, he can become free to grow beyond the gay-versus-straight mentality (that served him so well) and develop a more realistic view of the society around him and the conditions of his life.
—STANLEY SIEGEL, PSYCHOLOGIST, AND ED LOWE, JR.,
JOURNALIST, *UNCHARTERED LIVES*

My quietness has a man in it, he is transparent
and he carries me quietly, like a gondola, though the
streets.
—FRANK O'HARA, POET, "IN MEMORY OF MY FEELINGS"

The bliss that derives from oblivion is not a simple thing.
—TERRY ANDREWS, WRITER, *THE STORY OF HAROLD*

Our challenge of consciousness-raising is not limited to the heterosexually impaired but extends into our own ranks as well.

—CRAIG G. HARRIS, WRITER

Many times letting go means admitting you are not in control of life. If you were in control, you would not have suffered this loss; you would not have this pain; you would not have to remake your life to fill the void left by a friend who is no longer there. You can resolve to yourself, "Today I will allow myself to go on. I will experiment to see what new life could be like."

—LEONARD J. MARTINELLI, FRAN D. PELTZ,
WILLIAM MESSINA, AND STEVEN PETROW, WRITERS,
WHEN SOMEONE YOU KNOW HAS AIDS: A PRACTICAL GUIDE

My pain was the horse that I must learn to ride. I flicked my cigarette out of the window and watched it drop and die. I thought of throwing myself after it. I was no rider and pain was no horse.

—JAMES BALDWIN, WRITER, *TELL ME HOW LONG THE TRAIN'S BEEN GONE*

One must either accept some theory or else believe one's instinct or follow the world's opinion.

—GERTRUDE STEIN, WRITER, "HELEN"

I'm a person who's a woman, and I don't like dresses or panty hose or heels. I guess you could chuckle and say that I'm just a woman trapped in a woman's body. But, if you did say that, nobody would know what you meant, and probably more than one person would ask you to kindly stop chuckling.

—ELLEN DEGENERES, ACTRESS

Acting Up ... and Then Some

If AIDS has taught us anything, it is that we are the most tenacious, inspired, creative, caring, committed survivors on the face of this earth.

—RODGER MCFARLANE, AIDS ACTIVIST AND WRITER

Gay people who have AIDS are still our sons, our brothers, our cousins, our citizens. They're Americans too. They're obeying the law and working hard. They're entitled to be treated like everybody else.

—PRESIDENT BILL CLINTON

Queers are in a state of urgency. We are dying quicker than we are coming out. Will we be here in twenty years at this rate?

—SJORDAL@ZEUS.TOWSON.EDU, POSTED ON THE INTERNET

The notion of any illness being a punishment from God is not only ignorant but mean-spirited. Let us never descend to that level.

—ANN LANDERS, COLUMNIST

DON'T BE A FUCKING IDIOT.
—EDMONTON (CANADA) AIDS NETWORK'S PRO-CONDOM CAMPAIGN

I think they should change the name of this disease. From AIDS to AIDA. Only Leontyne Price can do it justice.

—SARAH SCHULMAN, WRITER, *RAT BOHEMIA*

I've seen a world vanish—a culture that has been oppressed in one generation, liberated in the next, and wiped out in the next.

—EDMUND WHITE, WRITER

I didn't come to Washington to be a faceless bureaucrat. I came to Washington to be a bureaucrat in your face. If a foreign enemy were killing that many people, we'd be calling out the Marines.

—BOB HATTOY, PRESIDENT CLINTON'S FORMER ADVISER
ON GAY ISSUES (HE CALLED HIMSELF "THE FIRST FAG")

If I'd known my blotches would turn purple, I'd have bought bags to match.

—STEPHEN SPINELLA, ACTOR, IN THE FILM *AND THE BAND PLAYED ON*

We're kind of like young men at war with this disease, where there's no cure and no vaccine.

—JIMMY SOMERVILLE, MUSICIAN

Silence = Death

—ACT UP SLOGAN

AIDS is this generation's Vietnam.

—RICHARD GOLDSTEIN, WRITER AND EDITOR

I want a man—but not a Negative any longer, not a man who's scared of the juices of my body. The Negative world is defined by fear, ours by pleasure—and it takes another Positive to treat me with the abandon for which sex was invented.

—SCOTT O'HARA, PUBLISHER, WRITER, AND FORMER PORN STAR

Despite what we know about AIDS, you just think people will never die.

—ANTHONY PERKINS, ACTOR

It's very hard for us not to cry out in anger, frustration, fear, desperation, and utter bewilderment: "How many people must die before something happens!"

—BOARD OF THE GAY MEN'S HEALTH CRISIS (1983)

All of us, people with AIDS and people without, are in this together.

—JOSEPH PAPP, THEATRICAL ENTREPRENEUR

AIDS doesn't go away when you turn off the television or close the newspaper.

—MICHAEL THOMAS FORD, AUTHOR OF
100 QUESTIONS & ANSWERS ABOUT AIDS

As someone who is himself HIV positive, I tend to avoid reading AIDS novels; the only thing I want to read is tomorrow's newspaper saying that a cure has been found.

—EDMUND WHITE, WRITER

Sometimes I'll do anything just to forget I'm wasting away.

—CYRIL COLLARD, WRITER AND FILMMAKER

AIDS . . . is an equal-opportunity merchant of death.

—GEORGE BUSH, FORMER PRESIDENT

When it comes to preventing AIDS, don't medicine and morality teach the same lessons?

—RONALD REAGAN, FORMER PRESIDENT

AIDS made me stop what I was doing and start to think about what I wanted, what I was doing to get it, what I could do differently, and who I am.

—PEDRO ZAMORA, HIGH SCHOOL STUDENT WITH AIDS

AIDS is everyone's problem, and everyone can be part of the solution.

—MERVYN F. SILVERMAN, M.D., M.PH., PRESIDENT,
AMERICAN FOUNDATION FOR AIDS RESEARCH

Is AIDS an atrocity in the sense that the Holocaust was an atrocity? The roles enacted by victim and villain are less clear—they may be one and the same. Repeatedly, we encounter the body as unreliable, as betrayer, and still unmistakably part of oneself.

—THOMAS AVENA, FOUNDER AND EDITOR OF *BASTARD REVIEW*

I don't want to be remembered as an old queen who died of AIDS.

—LIBERACE, PIANIST, ON HIS DEATHBED

Our bodies, even with AIDS, have enormous recuperative, regenerative, healing powers developed over millions of years of evolution. Let them be well.
—ROGER W. ENLOW, M.D., FIRST DIRECTOR OF THE NEW YORK CITY
OFFICE OF GAY AND LESBIAN HEALTH

I have lived for five years in a culture of disease, a small island in a sea of fear. I have seen many things there. I have seen how life speeds up and heightens in climates of extreme pain and emotion. It is hard to live in these circumstances, despite the acts of tenderness that can lighten everything. But it is also hard to pull away from the extreme, from life lived far from mundane conversation.
—ABRAHAM VEGHESE, DOCTOR AND WRITER, *MY OWN COUNTRY*

We must not let this awful sense of unknowing that AIDS yet represents divide us. We might all—each and every one of us—be potential AIDS victims. More than ever before we must fight together now—to help those who are already ill with AIDS, and to help insure our own future on this earth.
—BOARD OF GAY MEN'S HEALTH CRISIS (1983)

To live with this disease, to actually live and not simply survive it, means you're constantly engaged in some way with it. And it may not be AIDS directly that you're engaged with, but with all of the different struggles that are part of living, and being human.

—MARLON RIGGS, FILMMAKER

Perhaps the single positive contribution of AIDS to our culture is a politics of death. That is to say, AIDS (like the Right to Die movement) has made dying itself—in bed, away from the battleground—a political act.

—CAROL MUSKE, POET

I've been HIV-positive all my adult life. Everything I've accomplished I accomplished as an HIV-person.

—SEAN STRUB, FORMER PUBLISHER OF *POZ*

Problem: AIDS
Probable Cause: Denial of the self. Sexual guilt. A strong belief in not being "good enough."
New Thought Pattern: I am a Divine, magnificent expression of life. I rejoice in my sexuality. I rejoice in all that I am. I love myself.
—LOUISE L. HAY, AUTHOR AND LEADER IN THE NEW AGE MOVEMENT, *YOU CAN HEAL YOUR LIFE*

Our lives in the past decade and a half have become thoroughly imbued with AIDS and grief—it only follows that our sexual fantasies would also become intertwined with the complicated emotions surrounding sexual danger, the specter of death, and disease.
—JOHN PRESTON, WRITER, *FLESH AND THE WORD 3*

We die of AIDS every day and it's not acknowledged. Women need to be of equal priority.
—KRISTEN STUENKEL, PROTESTER OUTSIDE U.S. DEPARTMENT OF HEALTH AND HUMAN SERVICES

At least you haven't lost your sense of tumor.
—BRONSON PINCHOT, ACTOR, IN THE FILM *IT'S MY PARTY*

If you've got AIDS, you can come into this country. If you've got fruit, you can't. Do you understand this?
—JACKIE MASON, COMIC

AIDS is a test of who we are as a people. When future generations ask what we did in the war, we have to be able to tell them that we were out here fighting. And we have to leave a legacy to the generations of people that come after us. Remember that someday the AIDS crisis will be over. And when that day has come and gone there will be people alive on this earth—gay and straight people, Black people and white people, men and women—who will hear the story that once there was a terrible disease, and that a group of people stood up and fought and in some cases died so that others might live and be free.
—VITO RUSSO, FILM HISTORIAN AND GAY ACTIVIST

I Don't Like You and I Don't Like Your Poodle!

Homophobia: The irrational fear that three fags will break into your house and redecorate it against your will.

—TOM AMMIANO, COMIC

Most gay bashers will be wearing what gay people had on four years earlier—only in polyester with a Penney's label.

—PAUL RUDNICK, PLAYWRIGHT AND SCREENWRITER

It may be an academically interesting puzzle as to why we are gay . . . but it is much more interesting and important to find out why people are homophobic.

—PROFESSOR PETER NARDI, GLAAD/LA

Homophobia and Nuclear Power—Two Things We Can Do Without
—SIGN AT 1987 MARCH ON WASHINGTON FOR GAY AND LESBIAN RIGHTS

Native always means people who belong somewhere else, because they had once belonged somewhere. That shows that the white race does not really think they belong anywhere because they think of everybody else as native.
—GERTRUDE STEIN, WRITER, *EVERYBODY'S AUTOBIOGRAPHY*

I considered myself without shame: albinos aren't reproached for having pink eyes and whitish hair; why should they hold it against me for being a lesbian?
—NATALIE BARNEY, SAPPHIST OF THE BELLE EPOQUE

We need to purge male chauvinism, both in behavior and in thought among us. Chick equals nigger equals queer. Think it over.
—CARL WITTMAN, GAY ACTIVIST, *A GAY MANIFESTO*

People in my business don't trust straight people. There's a reverse snobbery.

—ISAAC MIZRAHI, CLOTHING DESIGNER

We call for the end of bigotry as we know it. The end of racism as we know it. The end of child abuse in the family as we know it. The end of sexism as we know it. The end of homophobia as we know it. We stand for freedom as we have yet to know it. And we will not be denied.

—URVASHI VAID, ACTIVIST

And this gay stuff in the military. Leave gay people alone. Let them do their thing, man. Fuck that. You know what I'm saying, they should be able to fight in the war just like any-fucking-body else. It's their thing, you know, they march and they shit. Them good motherfuckin' soldiers, 'cause they emotional with this shit. I bet they coming-home party a motherfucker.

—MARTIN LAWRENCE, COMIC, *YOU SO CRAZY*

Black bodies in this society have for centuries been a subject of Western repulsion, obsession, and revulsion. The black community has internalized that.
—MARLON RIGGS, FILMMAKER

Enemy=anyone with any type of homophobia or heterosexism. I advocate the extermination of heterosexual culture, not of heterosexuals.
—SJORDAL@ZEUS.TOWSON.EDU, POSTED ON THE INTERNET

If you are a bigot, you can stereotype a sea of bodies marching down the street. But when you look at an individual human being in the eye, you have to deal with him.
—MARLA STEVENS, HEAD OF NGLTF'S CAPITOL HILL LOBBYING EFFORT

Discriminating against people on their genetic makeup is wrong. That's as true when the genes in question affect sexual orientation as it is when the genes determine skin color.
—DEAN HAMER, GENETICIST, AND PETER COPELAND, *THE SCIENCE OF DESIRE*

We're still dealing with a world filled with lovable hillbillies, the ones who don't understand homosexuality and won't open their minds to live and let live.
—LORNA LUFT, MUSICIAN AND DAUGHTER OF JUDY GARLAND

You just can't say lesbianism hurts women's golf. It's more correct to say homophobia does.
—DONNA LOPIANO, EXECUTIVE DIRECTOR OF
THE WOMEN'S SPORTS FOUNDATION

Regarding homophobia in general, the good news is that there is a lot less of it than there used to be. The bad news is that it ever existed in the first place, and the worse news is that it remains far stronger than is healthy for a society dedicated in theory to equality under the law.
—BARNEY FRANK, U.S. REPRESENTATIVE

Military authorities are prohibited under the First Amendment from expelling soldiers who are members of extremist hate groups, as long as their membership is not "active." Under today's regulations, therefore, a soldier who tells his commanding officer, "I am gay," will be automatically discharged, whereas a soldier who tells a superior, "I am a member of the American Nazi Party and a believer in the ideals of Adolf Hitler," will be allowed to serve.

—EDITORIAL IN *THE NEW REPUBLIC*, DECEMBER 27, 1995

We recognized oppression as oppression, no matter where it came from.

—YVONNE FLOWERS, ACTIVIST

If we—and now I mean the relatively conscious whites and the relatively conscious blacks, who must, like lovers, insist on, or create the consciousness of others—do not falter in our duty now, we may be able, handful that we are, to end the racial nightmare, and achieve our country, and change the history of the world.

—JAMES BALDWIN, WRITER, *THE FIRE NEXT TIME*

O'er the Ramparts

We are not alone. There will be ups and downs, progress and setbacks. Throughout it all: We rise.
—GABRIEL ROTELLO, JOURNALIST

We have cooperated for a very long time in the maintenance of our own invisibility. And now the party is over.
—VITO RUSSO, FILM HISTORIAN AND GAY ACTIVIST

What use to us are laws of right and wrong?
—CHARLES BAUDELAIRE, POET

As leaders . . . we could not display fear. In the process we overcame our fears.
—DEL MARTIN AND PHYLLIS LYON, LESBIAN ACTIVISTS, *LESBIAN/WOMAN*

Feminism is the theory and lesbianism is the practice.
—TI-GRACE ATKINSON, WOMEN'S RIGHTS ACTIVIST

Take a Lesbian to Lunch.
—RITA MAE BROWN, WRITER, TITLE OF ESSAY WRITTEN IN REACTION TO
ANTIGAY ATMOSPHERE OF THE NATIONAL ORGANIZATION FOR WOMEN

Society knows very well how to go about suppressing a
man and has methods more subtle than death.
—ANDRÉ GIDE, WRITER, *IN MEMORIAM OSCAR WILDE*

Deciding which contingent to march with at the annual
gay pride parade in your city can be as difficult as
deciding what to bring to the next potluck.
—LYNN WITT, SHERRY THOMAS, AND ERIC MARCUS,
EDITORS OF *OUT IN ALL DIRECTIONS*

When the bigots came it was time to fight, and fight we
did. Fought hard—femme and butch, women and men
together.
—LESLIE FEINBERG, WRITER AND GENDER ACTIVIST

You should never be anything but harsh and confrontational with every drug company.
—LARRY KRAMER, WRITER AND AIDS ACTIVIST

Gay people have a different role than other minority groups. A lot of minority groups have had to fight for their political rights, but they haven't had to fight as hard as we have for their identity, for having their existence acknowledged.
—U.S. CONGRESSMAN BARNEY FRANK

What would happen if, for one day, no queers bought anything from straight-owned businesses? No gas, no food, no nothing. What would happen if, one day, all queers just took off from work? Just took our $ and man/womanpower away and channeled it into our community. What would happen if we stopped thinking about "diversity" and started thinking about ourselves? Would we be better for it?
—SJORDAL@ZEUS.TOWSON.EDU, POSTED ON THE INTERNET

Gay is Good.

—FRANKLIN KAMENY, EARLY GAY ACTIVIST

Jokes don't kill people; what they kill is certainty, and activists can never forgive funnymen for this. To those hungry for progress, doubt is as welcome as modesty in a whore; but, while faith is nice, doubt gets you an education.

—JOHN LAHR, WRITER

Each time a woman begins to speak, a liberating process begins, one that is unavoidable and has powerful political implications.

—MARIANA ROMO-CARMONA, WRITER

I am also saying that a war of fighting is like a dance because it is all going forward and back, and that is what everybody likes they like that forward and back movement, that is the reason that revolutions and Utopias are discouraging they are up and down. And not forward and back.

—GERTRUDE STEIN, WRITER, *EVERYBODY'S AUTOBIOGRAPHY*

What disturbs me is how gay men all over this country can sit around with their friends dying, their lovers dying, their lives threatened, and not get off their asses and be activists again. Do they have a death wish? What's the matter with them?

—VITO RUSSO, FILM HISTORIAN AND GAY ACTIVIST

HOW DARE YOU MAKE MY LIFE A FELONY.

—SIGN HELD AT 1987 SANDRA DAY O'CONNOR SPEECH

The workplace, in which we spend more than half our waking lives, is rapidly emerging as the frontier of lesbian and gay activism.

—JAMES D. WOODS, ASSISTANT PROFESSOR OF COMMUNICATIONS, *THE CORPORATE CLOSET*

Lesbianism, politically organized, is the greatest threat that exists to male supremacy.

—RITA MAE BROWN, WRITER

We are Queer! We are Asian! We are all across the nation!

—CHANT OF SALDA (SOUTH ASIAN LESBIAN AND GAY ASSOCIATION)

The goal of activism is to give people resources for making their own decisions and leading their own lives. Activists can motivate other gay men, not control them or dictate to them.

—AIDS PREVENTION LEAGUE

We are right at the point of being able to turn things around in this country. But we won't do it unless gays and lesbians get out there and work on it. They aren't going to give it to us.

—KENNETH POMMERENCK, VETERAN

I advocate Queer Unity at all costs. I would never rob another queer or beat up another queer, etc. I look at queers as my brothers and sisters regardless of whether or not they are virtuous.

—SJORDAL @ZEUS.TOWSON.EDU, POSTED ON THE INTERNET

At a time when some question the need for a strong lesbian and gay culture, we say we want to keep telling our stories our way. It is an act of transgression which continues to be essential to the cultural health of a diverse society. It is an act of political significance which is essential to gay men and lesbians.

—BEV LANGE, PRESIDENT OF THE 1996 SYDNEY (AUSTRALIA) GAY AND LESBIAN MARDI GRAS

We younger Negro artists who create now intend to express our individual dark-skinned selves without fear or shame. If white people are pleased, we are glad. If they are not, it doesn't matter. We know we are beautiful. And ugly too. The tom-tom cries and the tom-tom laughs. If colored people are pleased, we are glad. If they are not, it doesn't matter either. We build our temples for tomorrow, strong as we know how, and we stand on top of the mountain, free within ourselves.

—LANGSTON HUGHES, POET

Breeders think they are gonna rule . . . I know what I'm gonna fuckin' do, Me & my queer friends are gonna barge on through! Riot queers are coming . . . so FUCK YOU!
—SJORDAL@ZEUS.TOWSON.EDU, POSTED ON THE INTERNET

Queerness in all its varieties flourished beyond human reckoning.
—JACK FERTIG ON TWENTY-FIFTH ANNIVERSARY OF STONEWALL, 1994

You Got to Have Friends

When people have asked me in the past if I'm gay. I've said. "I'm not gay, but I am festive."

—SHARON GLESS, ACTRESS

You always have to remember—no matter what you're told—that God loves all the flowers, even the wild ones that grow on the side of the highway.

—CYNDI LAUPER, MUSICIAN

In recent interviews . . . with the gay media, to my surprise, it's been put to me that I might be gay. . . . I found myself curiously flattered by this.

—PATRICK STEWART, ACTOR

There's nothing wrong with being gay, so to deny it is to make a judgment.

—KEANU REEVES, ACTOR

I think it's interesting that when you play a lesbian, people ask you if you're a lesbian, but if you play a serial killer, nobody asks you if you're a serial killer.

—NORA DUNN, ACTRESS

They say I'm "flaunting an openly homosexual lifestyle," as if there fucking is one. That really gets me. . . . Aren't we just talking about people loving each other? It's so fucking beyond boring.

—ROSEANNE, ACTRESS

Whoever you are, I've always depended on the kindness of strangers.

—TENNESSEE WILLIAMS, PLAYWRIGHT, *A STREETCAR NAMED DESIRE*

But death—Their deaths have left me less defined:
It was their pulsing presence made me clear.

—THOM GUNN, POET, "THE MISSING"

In a way, I think this is making me a better, more tolerant person. One thing about prejudices—once you break one of them, you're screwed, because then they all have got to go.

—CHER, ON HER DAUGHTER CHASTITY'S LESBIANISM

Before the flowers of friendship faded friendship faded.

—GERTRUDE STEIN, WRITER

I think an orgasm is your thing, and you should fuck whoever the fuck you feel like fucking. Whoever makes you come the hardest, that's who you should be with. And all those people who say you shouldn't do that, fuck them, because it ain't their fucking business.

—EDDIE MURPHY, ACTOR, FROM *PLAYBOY* INTERVIEW

There is not a scrap of truth that I am having an affair with my secretary. If I were a homosexual, these are not the times to hide it. I would say "yes."

—BRIGITTE NIELSEN, ACTRESS

I love gay people. I believe I was the founder of gay. I'm the one who started to be so bold, tellin' the world! You got to remember my dad [threw me] out me of the house because of that. . . . I was wearing makeup and eyelashes when no men were wearing that.

—LITTLE RICHARD, MUSICIAN

The conservative movement is founded on the simple tenet that people have the right to live life as they please, as long as they don't hurt anyone else in the process. No one has ever shown me how being gay or lesbian harms anyone.

—FORMER SENATOR BARRY GOLDWATER

I'm straight, but I'm not narrow.

—CYBILL SHEPHERD, ACTRESS

Dear Miss Manners:
What am I supposed to say when I am introduced to a homosexual "couple"?
Gentle Reader:
"How do you do?" "How do you do?"

—JUDITH MARTIN, ETIQUETTE COLUMNIST

I learned too well what it means to be a people, learned in the joy of my best friend what all the meaningless pain and horror cannot take away—that all there is is love.
—PAUL MONETTE, POET AND NOVELIST

You're kidding. You really are queer. But you're so attractive.
—LESLIE ANN WARREN, ACTRESS, FROM THE FILM *VICTOR/VICTORIA*

Gov. REAGAN SAYS: SOME OF MY BEST FRIENDS ARE HOMOSEXUALS
—COVER LINE FROM AN ISSUE OF *MIDNIGHT*

Of the sainted Lord Kitchener Queen Victoria once said, "They say he dislikes women, but I can only say he was very nice to me."
—PAUL FUSSELL, WRITER, *THE GREAT WAR AND MODERN MEMORY*

Went out last night with a crowd of my friends
They must've been women, 'cause I don't like no men.
—MA RAINEY, MUSICIAN

If I had to choose between betraying my country and betraying my friend, I hope I should have the guts to betray my country.

—E. M. FORSTER, WRITER

My dearest friends
today I will sing with a clear voice
   to enchant you all.

—SAPPHO, POET

If my music were to help two gay people to fall in love, I'd be very happy.

—ALBITA, MUSICIAN

My gay audience is as important to me as my pumps. I don't feel whole unless I have on five-inch pumps. I don't feel whole unless I have a gay crowd.

—PATTI LABELLE, MUSICIAN

Look, I've never had a problem with homosexuality. As far as I am concerned, you can fuck a dead horse. As long as you didn't kill the horse, it's fine.
—HOWARD STERN, ACTOR AND RADIO PERSONALITY

Really, Jerry Falwell called me that? Ellen DeGenerate? I've been getting that since the fourth grade. I guess I'm happy I could give him work.
—ELLEN DEGENERES, ACTRESS

That's Life!

You got to get it while you can.
— JANIS JOPLIN. MUSICIAN. "GET IT WHILE YOU CAN"

I've always wanted my love life to be as simple as the Home Shopping Club.
— JAMES HANNAHAM, JOURNALIST

This odd domestic life—greased by drugs and easy-come, Easy-go—goes on, so naturally, so left alone.
— DAVID GROFF, POET AND EDITOR, "A SCENE OF THE CRIME"

This Western culture of ours tends to sacrifice the full range of experience to a lower common denominator that's acceptable to more people; we end up with McDonald's instead of real food, Holiday Inns instead of homes, and *USA Today* instead of news and cultural analysis. And we do that with the rest of our lives.
—KATE BORNSTEIN, GENDER ACTIVIST AND WRITER, *GENDER OUTLAW*

If you don't live the only life you have, you won't live some other life, you won't live any life at all.
—JAMES BALDWIN, WRITER

We're all fucked up, and we're not fucked up because we're gay. It's just because we're human.
—DANIEL MACIVOR, PLAYWRIGHT

Sex lies at the root of life, and we can never learn to reverence life, until we know how to understand sex.
—HAVELOCK ELLIS, SEXOLOGIST, *THE NEW SPIRIT*

Why go through life with one arm tied behind your back?

— JAMES DEAN, ACTOR

Life ain't the movies.

— DOROTHY ALLISON'S MOTHER, EVALUATING HER PAST, IN
TWO OR THREE THINGS I KNOW FOR SURE

We reach out our hands and they do not meet,
the space in between is our lives.

— GAVIN DILLARD, POET, "OUR LAST EMBRACE"

For some reason or other life is a piece of cheerie oats

— TAYLOR MEAD, POET, "ON AMPHETAMINE AND IN EUROPE"

The problem is isolation
—there in the grave
    or here in oblivion of light.

— ALLEN GINSBERG, POET, "SIESTA IN XBALBA"

The Future

If time holds a miracle
we'll dance together
as two old men

—BIL WRIGHT, POET, "MIRACLE"

Remembering how far we've come toward the goal of equality, as well as how far we have to go to reach it, both are essential if we are to get there.

—U.S. REPRESENTATIVE BARNEY FRANK

I told him my age—twenty—
and he expressed wild wonder
at all the sex ahead of me

—WAYNE KOESTENBAUM, POET, "1979"

Many will say it is a dream, and will not follow my inferences: but I confidently expect a time when there will be seen, running like a half-hid warp through all the myriad audible and visible worldly interests of America, threads of manly friendship, fond and loving, pure and sweet, strong and life-long, carried to degrees hitherto unknown.

—WALT WHITMAN, POET, *DEMOCRATIC VISTAS*

All different sexual persuasions, genders and races will continue to break new ground and challenge stereotypes. Individuality creates change: conformity slows progress.

—HONEY DIJON, DRAG QUEEN

Future-ex-old-man: ex-lover who can't be gotten out of the blood. "No, I can't say we really go together anymore; he's my future-ex-old-man."

—BRUCE RODGERS, *THE QUEEN'S VERNACULAR: A GAY LEXICON*

The hardest part about being a kid is knowing you have got your whole life ahead of you.

—JANE WAGNER, WRITER, *MY LIFE SO FAR*

Warriors of peace, we go hand in hand toward a world where all people can live as brothers and sisters. It is the beauty of our differences that gives us so much in common.

—BOB PARIS, BODYBUILDER

Probably Bill Clinton will not be reelected and will be replaced by a Reagan/Bush type of guy. Probably the Christian right will continue their already too successful campaign against us while the rest of America stands passively by. Probably the AIDS crisis will not end. . . . Probably, the nature of homophobia will never be widely interrogated, while we will continue to be excluded from school curricula, subjected to vicious media distortions, or entirely ignored, denied basic civil rights while our demands are ridiculed and derided. But in the midst of all this only one thing has changed for certain. We have changed. We will never go back into the closet.

—SARAH SCHULMAN, ACTIVIST AND WRITER, *MY AMERICAN HISTORY*

Good Advice
(and Then Some)

The truth is. when you're rich and bothered and restless. a hustler is easier to cope with than a sit-down dinner for six.

—ARTHUR BELL. JOURNALIST. *KINGS DON'T MEAN A THING: THE JOHN KNIGHT MURDER CASE*

Too few is as many as too many.

—GERTRUDE STEIN, WRITER, *EVERYBODY'S AUTOBIOGRAPHY*

You Got to Burn to Shine.

—JOHN GIORNO, POET

As long as the music's loud enough, we won't hear the world falling apart.

—DEREK JARMAN, DIRECTOR

If you are a human being, you might as well face it. You are going to rub a lot of people the wrong way.
—JANE WAGNER, WRITER, *MY LIFE SO FAR*

The mind of the bigot is like the pupil of the eye: the more light you pour on it, the more it will contract.
—OLIVER WENDELL HOLMES, JR., AMERICAN JURIST

A French egghead once said, "Ugliness is superior to beauty because it lasts longer." In other words, screw beauty.
—KEN SIMAN, WRITER, *THE BEAUTY TRIP*

Once the tables are turned, only a humiliator can appreciate humiliation's sweeter edges.
—TRUMAN CAPOTE, WRITER, *ANSWERED PRAYERS*

A man is not a man until he is able and willing to accept his own vision of the world, no matter how radically this vision departs from that of others.
—JAMES BALDWIN, WRITER

Everything in moderation . . . including moderation.
—ZDARKSTUD@AOL.COM, POSTED ON THE INTERNET

You should try a little muff now and then. I bet you'd forget all about being a faggot.
—BRUCE BENDERSON, WRITER, *USER*

Unless you are at a picnic, life is no picnic.
—JANE WAGNER, WRITER

Celebrate
Celebrate that morning follows night
Celebrate
Celebrate that wounded birds take flight
—BILL RUSSELL, DIRECTOR AND SONGWRITER, "CELEBRATE"

My mom says I have to be more positive, and I say life has to be more positive too or it's just not going to work.

—JANE WAGNER, WRITER, *MY LIFE SO FAR*

All the fairy tales have happy endings
Even though the passage can be rough.

—BILL RUSSELL, DIRECTOR AND SONGWRITER,
"I DON'T KNOW HOW TO HELP YOU"

Index

Index

Index